Mysterious Places

Mysterious Places

New and future titles in the series include:
Alien Abductions
Angels
Atlantis
The Bermuda Triangle
The Curse of King Tut
Dragons
Dreams
ESP
The Extinction of the Dinosaurs
Extraterrestrial Life
Fairies
Fortune-Telling
Ghosts
Haunted Houses
Jack the Ripper
The Kennedy Assassination
King Arthur
Life After Death
The Loch Ness Monster
Possessions and Exorcisms
Pyramids
Shamans
Stonehenge
UFOs
Unicorns
Vampires
Witches

The Mystery Library

Mysterious Places

John F. Grabowski

LUCENT BOOKS®

THOMSON
GALE

San Diego • Detroit • New York • San Francisco • Cleveland • New Haven, Conn. • Waterville, Maine • London • Munich

On cover: Stonehenge, Great Britain's ancient assemblage of stone megaliths, looms in the night under a canopy of stars.

LIBRARY OF CONGRESS CATALOGING-IN-PUBLICATION DATA

Grabowski, John F.
  Mysterious places / by John F. Grabowski.
    p. cm. — (The mystery library)
Contents: Stone sentinels—Earth etchings—Lost and abandoned cities—Pyramids and burial grounds.
  Includes bibliographical references and index.
  ISBN 1-59018-445-9 (hardcover : alk. paper)
1. Parapsychology and geography. 2. Sacred space. I. Title. II. Series: Mystery library (Lucent Books)
  BF1045.G46G73 2004
  001.94—dc22

                                                                  2004010202

Printed in the United States of America

Contents

Foreword

In Shakespeare's immortal play *Hamlet*, the young Danish aristocrat Horatio has clearly been astonished and disconcerted by his encounter with a ghostlike apparition on the castle battlements. "There are more things in heaven and earth," his friend Hamlet assures him, "than are dreamt of in your philosophy."

Many people today would readily agree with Hamlet, that the world and the vast universe surrounding it are teeming with wonders and oddities that remain largely outside the realm of present human knowledge or understanding. How did the universe begin? What caused the dinosaurs to become extinct? Was the lost continent of Atlantis a real place or merely legendary? Does a monstrous creature lurk beneath the surface of Scotland's Loch Ness? These are only a few of the intriguing questions that remain unanswered, despite the many great strides made by science in recent centuries.

Lucent Books' Mystery Library series is dedicated to exploring these and other perplexing, sometimes bizarre, and often disturbing or frightening wonders. Each volume in the series presents the best-known tales, incidents, and evidence surrounding the topic in question. Also included are the opinions and theories of scientists and other experts who have attempted to unravel and solve the ongoing mystery. And supplementing this information is a fulsome list of sources for further reading, providing the reader with the means to pursue the topic further.

The Mystery Library will satisfy every young reader's fascination for the unexplained. As one of history's greatest scientists, physicist Albert Einstein, put it:

> The most beautiful thing we can experience is the mysterious. It is the source of all true art and science. He to whom this emotion is a stranger, who can no longer wonder and stand rapt in awe, is as good as dead: his eyes are closed.

Explaining the Unknowable

Today, despite the increased pace of modern discoveries made possible through technological breakthroughs, mysteries that have intrigued man for hundreds—even thousands—of years remain unsolved. In some cases, new technology has even added to the mystery. Modern dating methods, for example, reveal that Stonehenge, long thought to have been built by the Druids, was built thousands of years before their time.

The massive monoliths at Stonehenge, the designs drawn on the plains at Nazca, the Inca ruins at Machu Picchu, and the Great Pyramid of Cheops at Giza continue to invoke awe in those seeing them for the first time. How could such majestic wonders have been constructed by primitive societies, some of which may not even have had a written language? How could such societies have developed the technologies needed to raise the stones found at Stonehenge and those used in the Great Pyramid? How could such huge blocks have been transported miles to their final destinations? As intriguing as such questions may be, even more puzzling in some cases are the reasons why such tasks were attempted in the first place. What caused the Incas to build a city high in the Andes mountains of Peru? Why did the Nazcans of the same country form line figures on the ground, figures that could not be deciphered except by someone situated high above them? Even mysteries of more recent vintage tantalize us. Why would someone go to the trouble of forming astonishingly complex figures in the fields of southern England, figures in some cases based on advanced mathematical models? Everyone loves a good mystery, and everyone loves to play detective. What could be more challenging than trying to answer questions that have stumped mankind for centuries?

Developing an Appreciation

The civilizations that produced wonders such as these have long since passed from this world. Since some had no written language, there is no way of knowing for certain the answers to many of these questions. What is clear, however, is that the dedication, the effort, the planning, and the

Despite extensive research utilizing cutting-edge technologies, precisely how and for what purpose the enormous stones of Stonehenge were erected remain a mystery.

teamwork involved in such constructions were staggering. This leads us to a better appreciation of the cultures responsible.

Perhaps even more remarkable is the fact that these wonders have survived at all. People have grown used to tearing down the old and replacing it with the new and do not always appreciate, respect, or even make an effort to maintain what has come before. In the twenty years following their discovery in 1940, for example, the ancient cave paintings at Lascaux, France, suffered more damage than in the previous seventeen thousand years since they were drawn. Graffiti can be seen on some of the monoliths at Stonehenge, and the Uffington white horse in England has been defaced with three white hounds and a rider added in biodegradable paint.

Such disrespect was shown by past civilizations as well. Mexican pyramids were covered with dirt and buried under newer buildings, monoliths at Avebury were broken up and used in the construction of homes in the village, and graffiti has sullied the megaliths at Stonehenge and Carnac. Unless more regard for the works of our ancestors is shown, future generations will have even more mysteries to unravel.

Chapter 1

Stone Sentinels

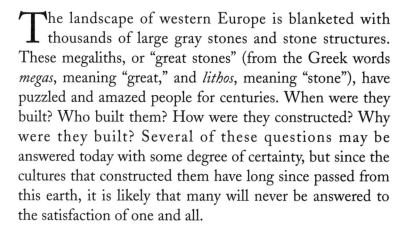

The landscape of western Europe is blanketed with thousands of large gray stones and stone structures. These megaliths, or "great stones" (from the Greek words *megas*, meaning "great," and *lithos*, meaning "stone"), have puzzled and amazed people for centuries. When were they built? Who built them? How were they constructed? Why were they built? Several of these questions may be answered today with some degree of certainty, but since the cultures that constructed them have long since passed from this earth, it is likely that many will never be answered to the satisfaction of one and all.

Out of the Distant Past

Megaliths abound in Europe, but they can also be found in other regions of the world. All told, an estimated fifty thousand megaliths exist today. Countless others have been destroyed over the years by forces of both nature and man.

The majority of these monuments can be found in western Europe, in a great arc extending from Sweden and the Shetland Islands in the north to Spain, Portugal, and Malta in the south. At one time, it was believed that these structures were imitations of monuments built by other cultures in the East. By the 1960s, however, more accurate methods of dating showed that many were built prior to those in the Aegean Islands, in Egypt, and in Mesopotamia.

Some in Brittany, a region in northern France, predated the Great Pyramid of Egypt by almost one thousand years, while others at Stonehenge had already been destroyed and rebuilt long before the Greek monuments came into existence.

Tantalizing Questions

Mysteries surrounding these magnificent stone monuments abound. What could their purpose be? Over the centuries, numerous theories have been proposed. Most megaliths are believed to have been used either for burial sites, astronomical observatories, or sites for religious ceremonies. Other theories suggest they may have been the scene of battles, sporting events, marketplaces, or even UFO bases. Many were thought to have supernatural powers and the ability to heal. Some people even believed fairies resided in some stones and the devil in others.

Since the majority of megaliths date back to the Neolithic period, the question is raised as to how they could have been quarried, using only the most primitive tools. Once quarried, how could these multiton behemoths have been transported—sometimes hundreds of miles—to their intended sites? Once there, how could such enormous monuments be raised erect and sometimes placed on top of other large stones?

Menhirs and Dolmens

These stone monuments vary greatly in size and shape but are generally grouped into three categories. The first, those made of single upright stones, are called menhirs (Celtic for "long stones"). These may weigh as much as several hundred tons. The largest known example, the Grand Menhir Brisé at Locmariaquer in the Brittany region of France, weighs 385 tons and once stood seventy feet high (it is now broken up into four pieces, possibly from being hit by lightning).

A second category consists of menhirs that are arranged in circles or rows. The best known of these is the circular formation of Stonehenge on the Salisbury Plain in Amesbury, England. The largest formation of stones stands at Carnac, also in Brittany. There, nearly one thousand stones are set in long, nearly parallel chains.

The final category of megaliths is composed of the roofed structures known as dolmens (Celtic for "table stones"). Bones and objects that appear to be offerings to

Rows of massive stone pillars known as megaliths stand in the French region of Brittany. Most of the megaliths found throughout the world date from the Neolithic period (5000–2000 B.C.).

the dead are often found inside dolmens, leading to the conclusion that many (though not all) were tombs.

Dolmens come in three basic varieties: single chamber, gallery grave or long tomb, and passage grave. As the name indicates, the single chamber variety consists of a small room with four stones for walls and another for a roof. The gallery grave is basically an elongated version of the single chamber tomb, with rows of stones for walls and slabs across the stones for a roof. The final form is the passage grave, which essentially combines features of the other two forms. A corridor as much as sixty feet long opens into a main burial chamber. This chamber is often round and is roofed with corbeling (overlapping stones that taper to form a domed ceiling).

Amazing Feats

The majority of megaliths are believed to have been built in the Neolithic period, between 5000 B.C. and 2000 B.C. The dolmens at Carnac, some of the oldest in existence, date back nearly seven thousand years. Since the cultures of that day were preliterate and had no written language, there exists no record indicating the purpose of these structures, or how they were built. What is certain is that the effort required to construct them was immense.

Using rudimentary tools such as picks made from the antlers of deer and shovels fashioned from the shoulder blades of oxen, huge boulders had to be pried out of the earth. Once exposed, some of the stones were hacked to shape them into rough cubes or circles, then inscribed with unusual designs; others were left in their original form.

The stones then had to be moved great distances, using nothing more than muscle power and perhaps domesticated oxen. When they arrived at their intended location, they had to be raised upright, probably by being wedged into holes dug in the earth and then lev-

Healing Stones

Over the centuries, a cult promoting the veneration of certain megaliths arose in England. The practice continued throughout the years, despite the efforts of the church to suppress it. One of the most popular reasons for this veneration of stones was the belief in their ability to cure certain diseases and afflictions. At Stonehenge, for example, the stones were washed with water. The water was then collected and poured into baths in which the sick were immersed.

It is believed the association of these stones with healing may have come from a confusion between the words "heal" and "heel" (possibly a corruption of the Greek word *Helios*, meaning "sun"). This may be found at Stonehenge, where the Heel Stone should more properly be called the Helios Stone, over which the sun rises at the summer solstice.

Stones with holes in them were especially associated with healing properties. Examples of these include the Men-An-Tol (also known as the Crick Stone) and the Tolvan Stone, both located in Cornwall, England. Those suffering from back, leg, and arm pain, and children suffering from rickets (a disease characterized by defective bone growth), were reportedly cured by climbing through—or being passed through—the hole several times.

ered into position. Finally, large stones had to be raised up to form the roofs and doorways of the chambers. The architectural planning and labor needed to complete these structures is incredible when considering the low level of technological development of their primitive builders.

How Were They Built?

Musing about Stonehenge around A.D. 1130, the English clergyman Henry of Huntingdon wrote in his *History of the English*, "Staneges, where stones of wonderful size have been erected after the manner of doorways . . . and no one can conceive how such great stones have been so raised aloft, or why they were built there."[1] Although it might be hard to imagine primitive peoples moving enormous stones great distances and raising them in such majestic works, it is certainly within the realm of possibility, even without the aid of the mythical magician Merlin who, according to

twelfth-century writer Geoffrey of Monmouth, "put together his own engines,"[2] which he used to help move the megaliths to Stonehenge.

The ancient world provides researchers with clues. One ancient Egyptian work of art depicts a gigantic statue carried on a sledge that is being pulled by some ninety men. The megaliths may have been moved in a similar fashion. Hundreds of men probably helped transport the stones, pushing them on wooden sledges over rollers carved from tree trunks. The stones were likely held in place by ropes made from vegetable fiber. These would be necessary in order to brake the momentum of the sledges as the stones were transported downhill.

Early attempts to explain how the megaliths of Stonehenge were transported and raised into place concluded that the monument is the work of supernatural beings and forces.

Once at the designated site, the stones had to be set upright. A deep hole with one slanting side was probably dug. The stone could then be maneuvered slowly into the hole. Once in place, it could be raised to a vertical position by men using a fulcrum and lever.

Raising slabs to cap the stones presented another problem. One way this could have been accomplished was by forming a structure made from logs next to where the stone had to be raised. As workers would pry up one end of the slab, logs could be shoved underneath it. The process would be repeated at the other end, then alternately from one end to the other until the stone was at the desired height. It could then be slid into position. Another method, suggests writer Robert Wernick, "may have been to drag them up a slope. With the uprights in position, hundreds of workers would set about piling earth and rubble to make a ramp against the standing stones. When completed, it would have formed an artificial hill on which stones could be hauled over log rollers."[3]

Who Were the Builders?

Because of the monumental size of the megaliths, early peoples attributed their construction to supernatural beings. Christians of the Middle Ages believed them to be the work of demons, wizards, fairies, natives of the lost continent of Atlantis, or ancient giants. In the *History of the Kings of Britain*, writer Geoffrey of Monmouth recounts tales that credit Merlin the magician for transporting the megaliths to Stonehenge from Ireland. More recent theories have attributed construction to the Druids, the Romans, the Phoenicians, and even aliens from outer space.

New technological advances, however, have enabled anthropologists to come up with more reasonable answers. Many of the monuments are tombs in which bones have been found. Examination of the bones indicates the remains are of the earliest inhabitants of the continent, which helps researchers determine who built these fantastic structures.

Why Were They Built?

Although scientists can speak with reasonable certainty about how the megaliths were raised and who built them, the reason for their construction is more puzzling. Some of the dolmens were tombs, but the purpose of the majority remains a mystery. It has been suggested they may have been the site of human sacrifices, tribal meetings, dances, feasts, marketplaces, or various religious ceremonies. Others have hinted they were monuments to great men or

The Ruins of Baalbek

Not far from the modern city of Baalbek in eastern Lebanon lie the ruins of a massive temple complex believed to have been built by the Romans in the late first century A.D. The complex consists of the Temple of Jupiter, the Temple of Bacchus, the Temple of the Muses, and the Temple of Venus. The massive Roman stonework, however, pales in comparison to the megaliths upon which it was built. This forms the largest stone-block construction the world has ever seen.

The platform of the magnificent Temple of Jupiter, called the Grand Terrace, has an enormous outer wall composed of twenty-four finely crafted and precisely positioned slabs weighing approximately 450 tons each. Atop the six blocks on the western side are three even larger stones called the Trilithon. Each of these is approximately sixty-four feet long and weighs at least one thousand tons. One still larger stone lies in a quarry a half mile away. Still attached to the quarry rock, it is the largest crafted stone in the world. Known as the Stone of the South, or the Stone of the Pregnant Woman, it is over seventy feet long and weighs an estimated twelve hundred tons.

The method used to quarry, transport, and place these huge rocks in position is a mystery to modern engineers and archaeologists. Given the amount of space in which they had to work, there is no known lifting technology even today that could have raised the stones into place. That it was done perhaps thousands of years before the Roman temples were added above it makes it all the more incredible.

A colonnade from the Temple of Jupiter at Baalbek still stands. The Roman temple sits on top of a much older megalith foundation.

tribal leaders. Still others believe they served as rudimentary astronomical observatories.

Whatever their purpose, it was important enough for the builders to devote a good portion of their lives to the completion of these constructions. This was possible, suggested British archaeologist Stuart Piggott, because the inhabitants of the region did not have to spend a great deal of time on other tasks, such as finding food. Wild game and farmland was abundant, leaving time for the months, the years, and even the decades of toil required to erect the megaliths. Stonehenge, arguably the most complex of these ancient structures, is believed to have been constructed in several different stages over a period of more than fourteen hundred years.

The "Giants' Dance"

The circle of stones known as Stonehenge is situated on the Salisbury Plain, about two miles west of the town of Amesbury, Wiltshire, in southern England. The name "Stonehenge," meaning "hanging stones," is attributed to the Saxons (a Germanic tribal group that inhabited northern Germany and invaded England in the fifth century). In medieval times, the megaliths were sometimes called the "Giants' Dance." They have fascinated man for centuries, as seen in the words Scottish philosopher Hector Boece wrote in 1527:

> To this day there stand these mighty stones gathered together into circles—"the old temples of the gods" they are called—and whoso sees them will assuredly marvel by what mechanical craft or by what bodily strength stones of such bulk have been collected to one spot.[4]

For many years, construction of Stonehenge was credited to the Druids. The Druids were the priests of the Celtic warrior class that populated England hundreds of years ago. Since they were believed to have magical powers, it seemed

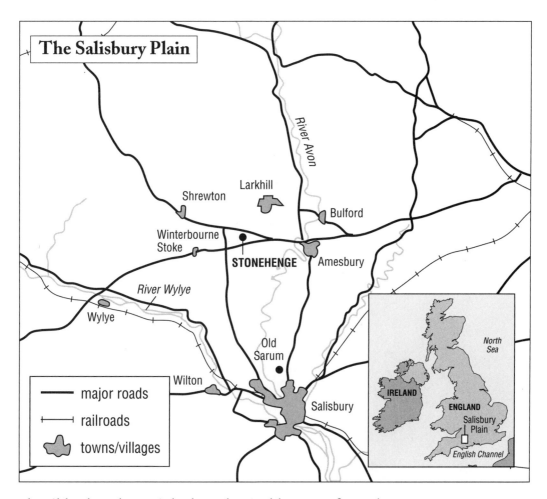

The Salisbury Plain

Shrewton
Larkhill
Bulford
Winterbourne
Stoke
STONEHENGE
Amesbury
River Wylye
Wylye
Old
Sarum
Wilton
Salisbury

North
Sea
IRELAND
ENGLAND
Salisbury
Plain
English Channel

major roads
railroads
towns/villages

River Avon

plausible that they might have been able to perform the monumental tasks necessary to construct the megaliths. It has since been determined, however, that Stonehenge was built long before the Druids were in the area.

Stonehenge I, II, and III

Although there is still debate about Stonehenge's intended purpose, researchers believe they know how it was built. Evidence unearthed after many excavations at the site has led archaeologists to conclude that Stonehenge was constructed in three distinct stages. In the first—Stonehenge I (started around 3000 B.C.)—a bank and ditch, or henge, as it was

Researchers speculate
that the thirty-five-ton
Heel Stone (foreground)
was erected during
Stonehenge's first phase
of construction, circa
3000 B.C.

called then, was dug in a large circle about 330 feet in diameter. Just within the circle was a ring of fifty-six holes, named Aubrey Holes after John Aubrey, the English antiquarian (someone who studies artifacts surviving from the past) who first discovered them in 1648. These holes were likely used to hold wooden posts. Also created as part of Stonehenge I was an earthwork avenue which runs through a break in the bank and ditch in the northeast corner of the circle. A slaughter stone was located at the break, and four station stones were erected in a rectangular pattern inside the henge. A thirty-five-ton heel stone was placed further down the avenue, outside the circle.

The second stage of the construction began around 2800 B.C. At this time, a double circle of eighty giant bluestones (igneous rock, mainly rhyolite and blue dolerite) was built within the henge. The entrance was widened and the avenue lengthened. Toward the end of this period, another group (the Wessex people) came into power and continued with the construction.

Stonehenge III, started around 2100 B.C., is further broken up into three substages (IIIa, IIIb, and IIIc). The central construction of thirty sarsens (large upright sandstone blocks) and five trilithons (crosspieces over two uprights) was erected at this time, with the trilithons forming a horseshoe. The sarsens were connected with lintels (large stones laid across the upright rocks) to form a circle. The central bluestones were dismantled early in this period, then later reerected. An altar stone was also raised in the center of the horseshoe.

The stones used in the construction came from many miles away—the sarsen stones from Marlborough Downs, twenty miles to the north, and the bluestones from the Preseli Mountains in southwest Wales, nearly 250 miles away. As Christopher Witcombe, a professor at Sweet Briar College in Virginia and an authority on Stonehenge, explained, "Clearly, a lot of trouble was taken by the builders to put those things up—and some of the stones were brought from a long way away. Which also . . . signifies how important that spot on Salisbury Plain must be if they went to all that trouble to get those stones to that particular place."[5]

Avebury Circle

Although Stonehenge is better known, the stone circle complex at Avebury in southern England is actually the largest in the world. Avebury is composed of a huge circular bank a mile in circumference, a massive ditch within the bank, a great ring of ninety-eight sarsen stones within that, and the remnants of two smaller circles of thirty stones each along with assorted other stones in the center. Much of the village of Avebury lies within the twenty-eight and a half acres enclosed by the fifteen-foot-high bank.

The stones at Avebury are not cut like those at Stonehenge but rather were left rough and irregular. Over the years, many were destroyed by farmers intent on clearing the region for fields of crops. Others were used in the construction of many of the village buildings. Still others were buried in the ground. Included among these is one large stone that unexpectedly fell into the pit being prepared for it, crushing a man. Years later, a pair of scissors, a lancet (surgical knife), and three silver coins were found next to his skeleton, giving the megalith its name of the Barber's Stone.

As with Stonehenge, the exact purpose of Avebury is not known. Its construction is believed to have begun around 2500 B.C. Because of the human remains that have been found, it is thought to have been a burial site. Animal bones that have been uncovered suggest it may also have been a cattle market or a site where pagan rituals were held.

The stones at Avebury form the largest stone circle in the world.

An Ancient Enigma

Today, more than four thousand years after its construction was first begun, Stonehenge's purpose remains a mystery. As Witcombe says, "The fact that it was built over a long period of time makes it difficult to know if it maintained the same function over the time period or not."[6]

Eighteenth-century British antiquarian William Stukeley believed Stonehenge was a temple, possibly a center for Druid rituals. British astronomer Sir Norman Lockyer also subscribed to the temple theory, but for him it was a temple to the sun. To many others, it appears to have been constructed with regard to some sort of celestial alignment. The main entrance to the circle faces the direction of the rising sun at midsummer. In the exact opposite direction, the setting sun in midwinter shines through the two uprights of the trilithon in the formation's inner horseshoe.

The theory that Stonehenge may have been used as an astronomical calendar was proposed more recently. Astronomer Gerald Hawkins went so far as to suggest it was a kind of primitive astronomical computer that could predict eclipses and track the movements of the sun and the moon across the heavens.

When all is said and done, author E. Herbert Stone's summation may be the best of all. Said Stone, "It may have been a Temple for some form of worship—or a Court of Justice—or a Hall for ceremonial meetings of tribal chiefs. All we can say with certainty is: '*We do not know.*'"[7]

The Stones of Carnac

Outside of Stonehenge, the standing stones of Carnac in the Brittany region of France are probably the most famous megaliths in the world. Most of the three thousand stones are arranged in eleven long avenues, spread out over a distance of two and a half miles. Legend has it they were formed when the early Christian saint and pope Cornély was being pursued by a legion of Roman soldiers across the countryside. When Cornély turned around to face them, he made the sign of the cross and they were turned into stone.

Although the standing stones are the best known of the Carnac megaliths, the area also has many dolmens and passage graves. Another type of burial ground to be seen is the tumulus, which is a huge mound of earth and stones that covers a burial site.

The Stones' Origin

Archaeologists today believe the formations at Carnac were created over a period of generations during the early, middle, and late Neolithic period. They are composed of some of the oldest megaliths still in existence. Over the centuries, however, many of the stones have been knocked over and damaged. When Scottish archaeologist James Miln carried out excavations in the area in the 1860s, only seven hundred of the stones were still standing. Since then, many have been reerected, although not necessarily in their original positions. Early photographs suggest that the current arrangement might be less haphazard than the original and that some stones might even have been reset upside down.

The rows of stones at Carnac were at one time believed to have been used as funeral procession ways. A recent theory of Scottish engineering professor Alexander Thom suggests the site may have been used to predict astronomical occurrences such as the frequency of eclipses. No one today knows the answer for sure. As Lord Taylor once stated, "Everything remains hypothetical about Carnac's mysterious monuments, except for the religious feeling that inspired their construction. . . . Only a deep and zealous faith could have inspired the idea and the means to erect huge lumps of stone towards the sky, forever the object of our amazement and admiration."[8]

Easter Island

Although the majority of megaliths are located in Europe, others can be found in various parts of the world, including Africa, Asia, Australia, North America, and South America. Easter Island, in one of the most isolated areas of the South Pacific, is home to massive stone statues which have fascinated and mystified visitors for years.

During an expedition in the South Pacific in 1722, Dutch explorer Jacob Roggeveen sighted a small, uncharted volcanic island on Easter Sunday. He named the island in honor of the day, but he could not land until three days later due to stormy weather. When he and the three sailing vessels under his command finally did so, they were astounded to see the natives gathered around enormous stone statues of figures, some of which were thirty feet tall. As he later wrote, "These stone figures caused us to be

The stones used in the formations at Carnac, France, number among the oldest megaliths still in existence, dating from the early Neolithic period.

filled with wonder for we could not understand how it was possible that people who are destitute of heavy or thick timber, and also of stout cordage [rope], out of which to construct gear, had been able to erect them."[9]

The problems faced in erecting the statues were enormous. The average figure was just over thirteen feet tall and weighed just under fourteen tons. The largest, however, was over thirty-two feet tall and weighed approximately eighty-two tons—the equivalent of almost a dozen full-sized elephants. (Another statue that never made it out of the quarry was seventy-two feet tall and weighed more than 150 tons.) How could a primitive people, using only the most

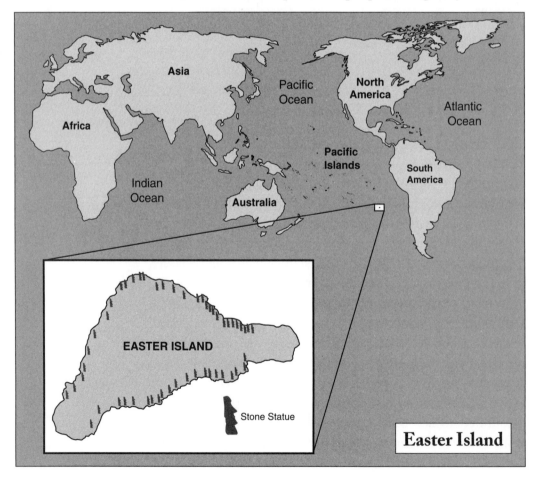

Easter Island

basic tools, move these immense objects to their intended sites, raise them erect atop the ceremonial *ahu*, or platforms, then top them with a red stone "topknot"?

Perhaps even more perplexing were the questions of who had built them and how had they reached the island. Located twenty-three hundred miles off the west coast of Chile, Easter Island is one of the most isolated spots in the Pacific Ocean, more than one thousand miles from its nearest neighbor, Pitcairn Island. Were the builders members of a race of ancient Polynesians, the ancestors of people who traveled from South America thousands of miles away, or perhaps extraterrestrials from a distant planet?

Hanau Eepe and Hanau Momoko

Roggeveen believed that about five thousand natives inhabited the island. These were composed of two groups: the Hanau Eepe, or "long ears" (so-called because their ears had been stretched out from wearing large ornamental wooden plugs in their lobes), and the Hanau Momoko, or "short ears." The statues seem more to resemble the Hanau Eepe.

Over the ensuing years, the island's population dropped precipitously. By the time British explorer James Cook visited in 1774, it stood at no more than seven hundred. The two factions had apparently been engaged in a drawn-out civil war that had decimated the island. The victorious "short ears" had wreaked their vengeance by destroying many of the statues—known as *moai*—of their enemy. In later years, the population dropped even further as other islanders fell victim to parties of Peruvian slavers. Included among those enslaved was the island's king, Kaimakoi.

Lost Knowledge

Much of the knowledge and lore concerning the statues were lost with the enslavement—and later death—of Kaimakoi. Archaeologists and scientists have found nearly

The Great Balls of Costa Rica

Another mystifying example of ancient stonework sentinels is Las Bolas Grandes—or the Great Balls—of Costa Rica. These stone spheres were uncovered by workers of the United Fruit Company, who were clearing the jungles of the Disquís Delta for banana plantations in the 1930s. The workers came across scores of these balls, ranging in size from several inches in diameter to more than eight feet, and from several pounds in weight to more than sixteen tons.

It was not until the 1940s, however, that the stones drew the attention of American archaeologists. Dr. Samuel Lothrop of the Peabody Museum at Harvard University discovered the spheres decorating the lawns of many private homes in the delta region. This made it hard to get an accurate count of how many balls there were, but it seems likely the number was in the hundreds.

The balls of Costa Rica are clearly man-made. The granite from which they were formed was not found in the Disquís Delta; it was likely transported many miles. The majority of the stones are almost perfectly spherical. Lothrop believed they were formed by grinding down large rocks with an abrasive made from sand and water. This abrasive was pressed into the surface with another stone. Because the stones were so perfectly spherical, Lothrop theorized they were carved with the use of some sort of template. Once the stones were formed, they were either dragged or carried to the delta, where they were placed in a variety of positions and locations. Smaller ones were often placed in graves, with larger stones arranged in long lines or sometimes triangles.

Although there is general agreement among most archaeologists about how the spheres were formed, their purpose is more of a mystery. Some believe they were nothing more than grave markers, while others consider them to be representations of the sun and the planets of the solar system. Since there was no mention of them in the early histories of Costa Rica, however, all such theories are pure conjecture. As one local archaeologist admitted, "If anyone knows about it, we do—and we know nothing."

nine hundred statues in various stages of completion. Approximately three hundred finished *moai* were overturned or destroyed during the warfare between the two groups. Others were found at different locations around the island, including nearly three hundred on the slopes of the Rano Raraku volcano in the east.

The completed statues stand on stone altars called *ahu*. The largest figure is thirty-two feet tall and weighs ninety tons. They have large heads, with brooding expressions on their faces. The heads—with their elongated, jutting chins—rest atop legless trunks. Arms are held stiffly at their sides. The enigmatic figures were described by French writer Pierre Loti, who visited the island in 1870. "What race did they represent," wrote Loti, "with their turned-up noses and their thin lips thrust forward in an expression of disdain or mockery? They have no eyes, only deep cavities under their large, noble foreheads, yet they seem to be looking and thinking."[10]

Visitors from Afar

Who, indeed, were the Easter Islanders? Because of the existence of the sweet potato on the island, some believed the original inhabitants came from South America, where the vegetable originated. In addition, stone walls on the island resembled Inca workmanship visible in Peru. Norwegian archaeologist and adventurer Thor Heyerdahl believed the original Easter Islanders had voyaged west from Peru, even though they would have had to cross thousands of miles of open ocean. In order to test the validity of his theory, he constructed a simple wooden raft—the *Kon Tiki*—and sailed from South America. He completed the trip to the Polynesian island of Puka Puka in 101 days.

Most archaeologists today, however, believe the island's first inhabitants came from the islands of Polynesia to the west. This, however, fails to explain Roggeveen's early reports of both light- and dark-skinned peoples living together. He even noted some as having red hair, which would not fit the Polynesian origin scenario. This might best be explained by still another theory.

Basque Ancestors?

Around 1536, a Spanish ship manned by Basque sailors was reported lost near the island of Tahiti. According to legend, the ship's survivors intermarried with the Polynesian islanders. At some future time, they tried to return home. However, they disappeared and were never heard from again.

Nearly nine hundred massive stone statues stand on Easter Island. Archaeologists have been unable to identify with certainty the identity of those who built these structures.

Centuries later, some pure-blooded native Easter Islanders were subjected to genetic testing. The testing revealed the presence of Basque genes, suggesting they might have been descendants of the lost Spanish seafarers, who had reached and colonized the island. Scientists will likely never know the final answer, and the builders of the mystifying stone figures will continue to intrigue people for years to come.

Whatever impulse caused ancient peoples to raise the mighty megaliths was not limited to one region of the world. The desires to honor the dead, to denote sacred sites, and perhaps to decode the mysteries of the heavens seem to be universal in scope. Cultures the world over have devoted years of work in order to raise these monuments. Although many have been destroyed through the centuries, thankfully many still remain as tributes to the efforts required to fulfill their creators' visions.

Chapter 2

Earth Etchings

In addition to the numerous mountains, rivers, forests, deserts, oceans, jungles, plains, and other natural features that adorn the surface of our planet, there are countless more that have been inscribed by the hand of man. Lines, circles, geometric shapes, and figures of every imaginable type can be found if one knows where to look. How, when, and why these figures were drawn, cut, or carved is often a mystery.

Pictures on the Earth

Located on the Nazca plains of southwest Peru, between the coastline and the Andes mountains, is a truly baffling sight. Huge geometric shapes and animal figures are etched into the desert surface. The figures, however, are indecipherable from ground level. They can only be seen from the air. The mystery of why these figures were drawn is considered by many to be among the most perplexing riddles of the archaeological world.

Geoglyphs and Biomorphs

For countless years, travelers to the Nazca plains undoubtedly noticed strange artificial markings in the ground. Where the omnipresent darkened stones had been removed, the lighter colored subsoil beneath was revealed. In this way, lines both straight and curved were formed covering a two-hundred-square-mile area. How these were formed is no mystery. As Dr. Persis B. Clarkson of the University of Winnipeg said, "It was not a difficult technology . . . all you need is the will."[11] With little rain or wind to erode them due to the extremely dry climate (Nazca averages about a half inch of rain every two years), the lines have remained throughout the centuries.

It was not until the 1920s, however, that the mysterious lines were revealed to be parts of more elaborate designs or figures. At that time, commercial airlines began flying over the area, treating passengers to the unexpected sights on the ground. What they saw were glimpses of approximately

The mystery behind the etchings of the Nazca plains of Peru (pictured is an outline of a pair of hands) is compounded by the fact that they can only been seen from the air.

nine hundred geoglyphs—geometric forms consisting of straight lines, triangles, circles, trapezoids, and spirals—and seventy biomorphs—animal and plant figures including a spider, a pelican, a hummingbird, a monkey, a lizard, and a tree. As archaeologist Maria Reiche described them years later, "Throughout the pampa [prairie], lines stretch for miles, crossing valleys and traversing hills, never swerving from their courses. Surveyors have been astonished by their straightness."[12]

The first person to study the lines was Peruvian archaeologist Mejía Xesspe in 1927. Fourteen years later, Dr. Paul Kosok of Long Island University became the first American to seriously study the designs, what he referred to as "the largest astronomy book in the world."[13] Kosok theorized that the markings were part of a giant astronomical calendar. He came to this conclusion as he and his wife watched the sun setting almost exactly over the end of one of the lines. Kosok later recalled, "Undoubtedly the ancient Nazcans had constructed this line to mark the winter solstice. And if this were so, then the other markings might very likely be tied up in some way with astronomical and related activities."[14]

Saint Maria

Kosok's work was eventually continued by a German woman named Maria Reiche. Reiche spent more than a half century at Nazca, so devoted to her work that the locals came to call her Saint Maria. Beginning with a grant from San Marcos University in Lima, Peru, Reiche took on the job of examining, recording, and helping to preserve the lines. Since many had grown faint over the centuries, she began cleaning the figures with a rake and a broom as she discovered and recorded them.

One of her discoveries was that the outline of the animal figures was executed with a single, narrow continuous line. This suggested that the figures might be ceremonial

Maria Reiche devoted more than fifty years to studying the Nazca shapes. Her work debunked the popular notion that the lines represent landing strips for extraterrestrials.

pathways. As art historian Alan Sawyer explained, "Most figures are composed of a single line that never crosses itself, perhaps the path of a ritual image. If so, when the Nazcas walked the line, they could have felt they were absorbing the essence of whatever the drawing symbolized."[15]

Alien Airfields?

Reiche also spent time debunking the theories of Swiss author Erich von Däniken. In his best-selling book of the

1960s *Chariots of the Gods?* von Däniken hypothesized that the Nazca lines were indications of an airport that had been used by extraterrestrials who visited the earth many centuries ago. (This theory had actually been proposed by other writers years before, and one publisher even contemplated filing a plagiarism suit against von Däniken.) He suggested the lines were runways and landing strips, and that some were created when the alien craft took off and landed.

Despite the popularity of von Däniken's book, his theories were generally rejected. As Reiche explained, "Once you remove the stones, the ground is quite soft. I'm afraid the spacemen would have gotten stuck."[16]

Early Flight?

Since many of the pictures at Nazca cannot be seen from the ground, there has been speculation that the Nazca Indians, who are thought to have made the drawings, were capable of some form of flight. This conjecture is supported by paintings of what may have been balloons or kites on pottery found in the area. In addition, circular pits of blackened rocks have been found at the end of many of the lines. These could have been launch sites for hot-air balloons.

One of those subscribing to this theory was American explorer Jim Woodman. In his book *Nazca: Journey to the Sun* Woodman explained, "I felt the people who built Nazca had to have seen it. It is all just too incredible to have never been

Ley Lines

In 1921 a respected Herefordshire businessman named Alfred Watkins was looking at a map of the local countryside. In a moment of inspiration, he noticed that various ancient points of interest, such as megaliths, burial mounds, and prehistoric earthworked hills, fell into straight lines that might stretch for several miles. He began to study these alignments in person and on maps, and in 1925 published his research in a book titled *The Old Straight Track*. He theorized that all holy sites and places of antiquity fell along these lines that he called leys, an Anglo-Saxon word meaning "cleared strips of ground." He believed they were the remnants of traders' routes laid out centuries before.

After Watkins's death in 1935, occult writer Dion Fortune suggested in her 1936 novel *The Goat-Foot God* that these were "lines of power" connecting prehistoric sites. A few years later, it was proposed that they, in fact, followed lines of cosmic energy in the earth and that they could be traced using dowsing rods (forked sticks that are said to dip down to indicate underground water).

Interest in ley lines died down over the ensuing period, then rekindled in the 1960s when UFO sightings were reported where these energy lines intersected. This eventually led to ley lines becoming part of the New Age movement associated with channeling, crystals, spiritual healing, and other phenomena outside the mainstream of scientific thought.

seen or admired by its creators."[17] In order to test his hypothesis, he and American Bill Spohrer assembled a balloon using only the materials and technology believed to have been available to the Nazcans. In November 1975, Woodman and copilot Julian Nott took off in the balloon—named *Condor 1*—and managed to stay aloft for about two minutes, reaching a height of three hundred feet. Although no evidence has shown that the Nazcans actually did fly, the trip showed it was theoretically possible.

There is no shortage of theories that attempt to explain the Nazca lines. In addition to those mentioned, others include their use as a kind of racetrack for a Peruvian version of the Olympics, as a memorial to a primitive cataclysmic war, as the remnants of early cultivated fields, and even as a vast textile workshop where immense strands of thread, some miles long, were woven into burial shrouds. As Sawyer said, "We can't be sure what their meaning was, but we can be sure they had meaning."[18]

The Crop Circle Controversy

An extremely large number of people do not think there is any meaning, other than mischief, behind the phenomenon of crop circles. A crop circle is an unexplained design that has been imprinted in a field over a brief span of time. To date, there have been approximately ten thousand of them reportedly sighted in over seventy countries around the world, with roughly 90 percent having appeared in Great Britain. Since many are hoaxes and have admittedly been man-made, many people doubt that the phenomenon is a mystery at all. To others, however, crop circles are a source of enduring fascination.

A Modern Phenomenon

Although there is some mention of crop circles as early as the seventeenth century, they are generally thought of as being a relatively modern phenomenon. The sighting

This crop circle appeared near a village in Hampshire, England, in 1991. Many of the crop circles reported throughout the world have been proven to be hoaxes.

that first garnered media attention occurred in southern England on August 12, 1972. The event was witnessed by Bryce Bond and Arthur Shuttlewood and described thus:

Suddenly, I heard a noise. It seemed as if something pushed down the wheat. That night the air was completely still. I looked around. The moon had just appeared, shining brightly. In front of my eyes I could see a great imprint taking shape. The wheat was forced down in a clockwise direction.[19]

Since that time, crop circles—or agriglyphs—have evolved from simple circles of relatively modest proportions into complex pictograms with dimensions dictated by complex mathematical formulas that can occupy as much as two hundred thousand square feet. Although the majority occur in fields of wheat or barley, they have also been found in fields of corn, oats, canola, grass, and other varieties of organic matter.

Changes and Transformations

Some researchers have reported finding changes in the plants and soil in crop circles. The plants are sometimes woven together in a particular way. They also may exhibit unusual bending, look dehydrated, have altered seeds, and appear to be changed at the molecular level. Biophysicist W.C. Levengood reports finding enlarged cell walls and extended node lengths in plants. Nodes are like small knuckles that allow plants to bend toward the light.

Levengood's results, however, have not been verified by other researchers. Many believe these changes are occasionally found in nature and have nothing to do with crop circles. Even Levengood himself admits, "Taken as an isolated criterion, node size data cannot be relied upon as a definite verification of a 'genuine' crop formation."[20]

Changes are not limited to the circles themselves. Scientists have associated high radiation levels and strange sounds with the phenomena. There have been reports of cell phones, cameras, and other electronic equipment malfunctioning when inside the circles and compasses spinning out of control. People standing in the affected areas have suffered headaches, nausea, tingling sensations, and dizziness. Even animals can be influenced, as one researcher found when his dog entered a circle. Reported Donna Yavelak, "The dog became violently ill and vomited for about an hour afterward."[21]

Scientists are pretty much at a loss when it comes to explaining these physical effects. They attribute some to magnetic fields and others to high heat or radiation. Some researchers simply say they are an unexplained natural phenomenon, refusing to accept any supernatural or otherworldly explanations.

Forces of Nature?

A variety of theories have been proposed to explain the existence of crop circles. These can be grouped into three general categories based on their implied origin: nature, humans, and aliens.

Since the first crop circles looked as if they had been swirled into the growing crops, many—including meteorologist Dr. Terence Meaden—believed they were caused by some kind of freak whirlwinds. As the figures became more complex and sophisticated, however, this explanation seemed less satisfactory. Meaden amended his theory to include superheated columns of air called plasma vortices. Other observers attribute their occurrence to magnetic fields, or naturally occurring force lines that radiate between the North and South Poles. Some go so far as to suggest that the earth itself is responsible for creating the formations as some sort of nebulous warning to mankind.

Farces of Man?

A great number of people believe crop circles are nothing more than a man-made hoax. They point to several characteristics that suggest the work of hoaxers. These include an increase in frequency (their number has increased, as has the media attention they have received); a fairly limited geographic distribution (the great majority have been reported in the southern part of England); an increase in complexity (designs have become more intricate, as if attempting to outshine those that came before); and avoidance of being observed (circles only seem to pop up at night, when an area is not under surveillance).

This crop circle with intricate geometric patterns appeared in Rockville, California, in 2003. Some attribute the complexity of crop circle designs to extraterrestrial intelligence.

The man-made theory was given a boost in 1991 when two middle-aged Englishmen named Doug Bower and Dave Chorley came forth to admit to the hoax. They claimed they were responsible for all the circles that had appeared in Britain, having created them by using a rope-and-plank device.

Interestingly enough, many people refused to believe them, asserting that the government put forward the two hoaxers in an effort to lessen interest in the growing phenomenon. According to Freddy Silva, author of *Secrets in the Fields: The Science and Mysticism of Crop Circles:*

> When confronted to provide evidence on certain claimed formations, Doug and Dave changed their story, even reversing previous claims; or they simply could not explain unusual features found in the genuine phenomenon. When they claimed making all the formations around the English county of Hampshire, for example, it was pointed out that half the known formations had actually occurred in another county.[22]

The skeptics' argument was further backed by data that suggest crop circles date back to the 1890s.

Aliens Among Us?

A more imaginative explanation attributes their existence to extraterrestrial forces. Hovering balls of light and other "energy" effects have been reported in the vicinity of crop circles on more than one occasion. A description of one such occurrence given by a witness is described in detail by author Linda Moulton Howe:

> It was so bright, it lit up the hills in the background. It was bluish-white in color and about as big as the formation, fifty to sixty meters wide. The bright light formed some sort of cloud and it changed shape continuously as it hovered over the formation.

After a couple of seconds, it rose at slow speed and disappeared into the darkness. My friend and I were totally flabbergasted![23]

People, too, have been flabbergasted by the intricate designs into which crop circles have evolved. The simple circles soon became connected with straight lines. Next were designs made up of more intricate patterns, some based on complex mathematical theorems. Such designs, say those who subscribe to the extraterrestrial theory, would require a very high degree of intelligence to produce. These theorists further speculate that only superior beings would have the advanced knowledge necessary to allow them to produce such figures on property such as fenced-in military grounds (as have been reported).

The crop-circle producers can apparently make their designs wherever they want, whenever they want. This unlimited mobility and degree of technical sophistication apparently rules out hoaxers or natural forces. It seems to indicate that whoever is behind the crop circles has a plan and is determined to put it into effect. Whoever this is, and whatever the plan may be, remains a matter of conjecture.

Hill Figures

Another kind of earth etching found in England is the hill figure. These large-scale drawings were created by cutting away turf to reveal the underlying chalky subsoil or bedrock. Cut into hillsides, the figures may be as large as several hundred feet in length and more easily seen from some distance away. In order to preserve them, they are sometimes scoured to prevent them from becoming overgrown.

There are believed to be approximately fifty hill figures still in existence, but the number is uncertain. Although it is sometimes hard to date them, there are references to hill figures as early as the eleventh century. Many are interpreted as religious and ritual symbols, possibly representing gods. Others are believed to have been sites that were important parts of ancient fertility ceremonies.

The Uffington White Horse

The Uffington white horse located in southern England is the most famous hill figure in the world. Many people associate the stylized figure with pagan deity worship.

Arguably the most famous hill figure of all, the Uffington white horse can be found on an escarpment of the Berkshire Downs below Whitehorse Hill, south of the village of Uffington. It is the oldest of the thirteen white horse figures that have existed in Wiltshire, eight of which are still visible. (Most of the others date from the last three hundred years

or so.) The horse was originally thought to have been cut during the Iron Age, but recent tests using optical stimulated luminescence dating have proved it much older. (In this method of dating, developed in the early 1970s, quartz or feldspar buried in the soil are examined to determine how long ago the grains were exposed to sunlight. Luminescence dating is especially useful when radiocarbon dating is not possible, as when no organic matter is present.) The first suggested reference to it occurs in a cartulary (collection of deeds or charters, usually to the property of an estate or a

monastery) of the Abbey of Abingdon from the eleventh century, which refers to "the place commonly known as the White Horse Hill."[24]

Unlike the other white horse figures found in Wiltshire, the Uffington white horse is a less naturalistic figure, consisting of long, stylized lines. Because of this sleek design, some people believe it represents the mythical dragon slain by St. George on nearby Dragon Hill. Others think it signifies the Celtic horse goddess Epona, who represents fertility, healing, and death. Still others believe it may have been cut by those who worshipped the sun god Belenus, who also was associated with horses.

No one knows for sure how old the horse is or why it is there. All that is known for certain is that the 374-foot-long figure was carefully tended to by

The Cerne Abbas Giant

Also known as the "Rude Man" because of its blatant sexual nature, the Cerne Abbas Giant is the largest hill figure in Britain. It measures 180 feet from head to toe, 167 feet in width, and is depicted carrying a knobbed club 120 feet long. According to legend, the figure represents a Danish giant who led an invasion of England. When he fell asleep on the hillside, the local villagers cut off his head and cut a line around his exposed body. Most historians, however, believe the figure was cut into the hillside between A.D. 180 and A.D. 193 during the reign of the emperor Commodus, who believed himself to be the reincarnation of Hercules. Still another theory attributes the figure to a joke played by the monks at a nearby monastery on an abbot who was forced to leave the abbey because of malpractice.

Because of the giant's obvious virility, fertility rituals often centered around the figure. Women who wished to conceive would spend a night alone on the hillside, as would young lovers hoping to ensure conception. Those wishing to keep their lovers faithful would walk around the figure three times.

local villagers for years. It has been ritually scoured, with the festive ceremonies accompanying the scouring coming to be known as the Uffington "pastime." The Uffington horse endures to the present day as testimony to the villagers' watchfulness, allowing future generations to form their own opinions regarding its origin.

Effigy Mounds

England is not the only country where figures of animals adorn the countryside. In the United States, several hundred effigy mounds—earthworks in the shape of animals and birds—can be found in parts of Wisconsin, Minnesota, Illinois, Iowa, and Ohio. Although most of these mounds have been identified as burial places, one is a particular source of mystery—the Great Serpent Mound that overlooks Ohio Brush Creek in Adams County, Ohio. When was it constructed and by whom? What does it represent? What was its purpose?

At more than thirteen hundred feet in length, the Great Serpent Mound is the largest effigy of a snake in North America. It averages four to five feet in height and twenty-five feet in width. The mound depicts a long, undulating snake with a coiled tail. It appears that the snake's mouth is open, about to swallow an egg. Some researchers, however, believe the "egg" is actually the reptile's head or eye, or even the sun.

A Disputed Origin

The Great Serpent Mound first came to the attention of researchers in the 1840s. It was generally believed that it was raised sometime between 800 B.C. and A.D. 1 by the Adena Indians, who are known as the Mound Builders because of the many earthworks they constructed. These works usually began as the grave of an individual, then grew in size as more burials were added to the site. The Great

At more than thirteen hundred feet long, Ohio's Great Serpent Mound is the largest effigy of a snake in North America.

Serpent Mound is unusual in that it was not used for that purpose. When Frederick Ward Putman of Harvard University first excavated the mound in the 1880s, he turned up shards of pottery, ashes, burnt stone, and some animal bones, but no human remains. The site became well known after he displayed his findings at the Chicago World's Fair in 1893.

Silbury Hill

Not too far from the stone circle at Avebury in southern England is Silbury Hill, the largest man-made mound in northwest Europe. The flat-topped hill reaches 130 feet high, covers an area of five acres, and contains approximately 12 million cubic feet of chalk. Legend has it that it was formed when the devil was forced to drop a huge bag of dirt he was carrying to pile on the town of Marlborough. Many believe the hill was the burial mound of King Sil, sitting on a fabled golden horse.

The hill has been excavated on three separate occasions. A shaft was dug from the top down to the middle in 1776, and tunnels were burrowed to the center in 1849 and 1968. The only things found inside were clay, turf, moss, flints, gravel, topsoil, shells, oak, hazel, mistletoe, sarsen stones (large sandstone blocks), ox bones, and antler tines.

Carbon dating has determined that the hill's construction began approximately forty-six hundred years ago. It was built in several stages, with six concentric steps, or ter-races, eventually being covered to form the cone-shaped mound. The entire construction took around fifty years to complete. As of today, the purpose of the hill remains unknown. One theory suggests it is a symbolic representation of the Mother Goddess and was associated with fertility rituals. Another explanation implies it could have been used as a solar observatory.

Nearly five thousand years old, Silbury Hill is the largest man-made mound in northwest Europe.

In more recent times, radiocarbon dating has suggested the mound was raised between A.D. 900 and A.D. 1200. If this is correct, it is more likely that the Fort Ancient culture, which thrived along the Ohio River and its tributaries, was responsible for its construction rather than the Adenas. The Fort Ancient people often used representations of snakes in their artwork.

A Multitude of Theories

Over the years, there have been several theories regarding the Great Serpent Mound. Ephraim Squire and Edwin Davis, the first to survey the site in 1846, believed it was an ancient Indian religious symbol. When first discovered, there was a fire-scorched stone monument in the oval "head." Some interpreted this as being some kind of altar. Since ceremonial knives were also unearthed in the region, along with several headless skeletons in nearby graves, it was theorized that the figure might have been the site of human sacrifices.

In 1885 John P. McLean published a map that depicted a mound in front of the oval, which he interpreted as a frog. McLean surmised that the snake was chasing the frog, which jumped away and ejected the egg. A completely different explanation was posited by the Reverend Landon West of Pleasant Hill, Ohio. West saw the figure as the snake from the biblical Garden of Eden. The oval mound represented the forbidden fruit from the tree of knowledge. The mound, said West, was created—or at least inspired—by God to mark the location of the Garden of Eden in Ohio.

A more recent theory, proposed in the late 1980s, takes into account the fact that the mouth of the serpent is in direct alignment with the setting sun on the summer solstice, the longest day of the year. This has led to speculation that the mound represents a solar eclipse. Researchers have since found that the outer curves of the creature align with

the rays of the sun at the four divisions of the solar year, adding further credence to the theory.

Still others have speculated that the figure was inspired by a supernova visible in the sky in 1054, or the brightest recorded passing of Halley's comet a dozen years later. Others suggest it is a model of the constellation known as the Little Dipper, with the snake's tail coiled about the North Star. Adding to the mystery are reports of strange happenings at the mound. These include unconfirmed appearances by the ghosts of the ancient Mound Builders. Perhaps they return to taunt those who are still trying to understand the significance of their work.

When viewed from above, the landscape of our planet reveals sights invisible or undecipherable from the ground. This fact makes such markings and shapes all the more mysterious. To attribute them to otherworldly forces only minimizes that which human beings are capable of accomplishing. The possibility of intervention by such forces, however, enhances the mystery surrounding the formation of these figures and forces us to open our minds to explanations that might be more unsettling than others.

Chapter 3

Lost and Abandoned Cities

There is perhaps nothing quite as eerie as a city without inhabitants. The silent array of buildings, towers, arches, monuments, and roads provides a ghostly aura to a scene repeated at numerous locations around the world. The likelihood that many of the questions concerning these ruins may never be answered only adds to the magic and the mystery.

Machu Picchu

In 1911 explorer and Yale professor Hiram Bingham set out to find the long-rumored "Lost City" of the Inca Empire in the Andes mountains of Peru. Outside the town of Aguas Calientes, a farmer named Melchior Arteaga told him about a settlement of ruins that lay high up in the Andes on a ridge between two mountains. He offered to lead him there in exchange for a few coins.

The next day, Bingham and the members of his expedition made their way through the jungle, then crossed some roaring rapids on a shaky bridge of four logs. They eventually made their way up toward a peak that towered high above the Urubamba River. After a long, strenuous climb,

Bingham came upon a series of beautifully constructed terraces. Walking along one of them, he suddenly found himself

Dating to the fifteenth century, the Inca city of Machu Picchu was built high in the Andes mountains without the benefit of draft animals or the wheel.

confronted with the walls of ruined houses built of the finest quality of Inca stonework. It was hard to see them for they were partly covered with trees and moss, the growth of centuries, but in the dense shadow, hiding in bamboo thickets and tangled vines, appeared here and there walls of white granite ashlars [square-hewn stones] carefully cut and exquisitely fitted together.[25]

Bingham had rediscovered the ancient Inca city of Machu Picchu ("manly peak" in the indigenous language).

Unanswered Questions

Further exploration of the ruins determined that Machu Picchu was composed of some two hundred well-preserved buildings, which included palaces, temples, tombs, and observatories. The surrounding mountainside was terraced for agricultural purposes, providing an area where maize and potatoes could be grown to feed the city's inhabitants. Parts of the city were connected by alleys, streets, and more than two hundred stairways carved into the mountainside. A series of narrow channels called *azequías* connected with a series of fountains, which supplied the city with water.

Machu Picchu posed many questions to Bingham and to the others who followed in his footsteps. Was it the legendary city of Vilcabamba? Who were the city's inhabitants? Why were 75 percent of the human remains that were found identified as female? Could Machu Picchu be a refuge for the Inca "Virgins of the Sun"? Why was it built in this particular area? Was it simply a city or did it have some other purpose? Why was it deserted? As Bingham wrote after examining the stone wall of one of the structures, "Dimly, I began to realise that this wall and its adjoining semicircular temple over the cave were as fine as the finest stonework in the world. . . . It fairly took my breath away. What could this place be?"[26]

An Engineering Marvel

The construction of Machu Picchu was a monumental enterprise. It is believed to have been built in the fifteenth century by the Incan ruler Pachacuti Inca Yupanqui. Incredibly, the complex of buildings was built without the use of draft animals or the wheel. The majority of the buildings were constructed of granite blocks, which were cut and

The majority of Machu Picchu's buildings are built with large granite blocks that were shaped with primitive tools to fit together perfectly.

shaped with the use of bronze or stone tools. They were fitted together so carefully that even now, hundreds of years later, not even a thin knife blade can be forced between them. As Bingham reported, they held "as tightly as a glass stopper fits into a glass bottle. Friction and an absolutely perfect fit do the trick."[27]

Construction was even more difficult owing to the site's location, some seven thousand feet above sea level, high above the Urubamba. This led some to conclude that Machu Picchu was a military garrison, providing the Incas with protection against the marauding forces of the Spanish conquistador Francisco Pizarro, who was ravaging Peru in his search for New World gold. If that was the case, however, it raised the question of why the city had been deserted. There is no archaeological evidence of any kind that the Spaniards ever reached the mountain fortress.

An Astronomical Observatory

One of Machu Picchu's functions was likely as an astronomical observatory. The site's most sacred object, according to most archaeologists, is the Intihuatana. The name of this column of stone rising from a larger block of stone is translated as "hitching post of the sun." The stone is an accurate representation of the shape of the surrounding mountains. It is believed that Inca priests held a ceremony during which they symbolically hitched the sun god Inti here during the winter solstice, when the sun seemed to disappear more each day. In this way, they hoped to ensure that it would return the next summer.

Inti was also honored at the building known as the Temple of the Sun. Archaeologists have determined that it is possible to predict the winter solstice when the sun's rays enter one of the building's two trapezoidal windows and touch the edge of the shaped stone inside.

Another Explanation

Newly uncovered evidence suggests Machu Picchu more likely was Pachacuti's royal estate. Just a three-day walk from Cuzco, this country palace would have allowed him and his royal court to escape from the pressures of daily life in the Inca capital. Because of its location high in the mountains, however, it almost certainly also had a religious significance. The Incas worshipped nature, and it is believed they considered Machu Picchu a sacred place imbued with *huaca*, or spiritual power.

When Pachacuti died, the retreat remained the property of his kinship group. It is theorized that it may have been abandoned when it became too costly to maintain, possibly magnified by the effects of a drought that made water scarce. Maintenance was made even more difficult due to the effects of an outbreak of smallpox that killed half of the Inca population by 1527. The existence of the retreat was known only to a select group of royals and religious figures. When it was abandoned, it was overgrown with jungle vegetation and soon forgotten.

Bingham's rediscovery of Machu Picchu in 1911 is considered by many to be the greatest archaeological find of the twentieth century. Situated high in the Andes mountains, it is one of the most breathtaking sites in all the world. For many who have visited Machu Picchu, it has become an almost mystical experience. As Chilean poet Pablo Neruda wrote in his epic poem "The Heights of Machu Picchu": "This was the habitation, this is the site, and now I am here. I am in awe."[28]

A Long-Forgotten Civilization

Not too far from Machu Picchu, about fifteen miles south of Lake Titicaca in the Andes mountains of Bolivia near the Peru border, lie the ruins of Tiahuanaco (or Tiwanaku), believed by many to be one of the oldest cities in the world and the "Cradle of American Civilization." At one time, it was thought to have been the home of the Inca Empire. Later excavations have proven it to be much older. Indeed, the city had already been destroyed long before the Incas even arrived. Sixteenth-century Spanish explorers were told by the Indians that "Tiahuanaco was built in a single night, after the flood, by unknown giants. But they disregarded a prophecy of the coming of the sun and were annihilated by its rays, and their palaces were reduced to ashes."[29]

Many of the ruins that remain do seem to have been carved by giant hands. Some have gone so far as to claim they are the work of aliens, or members of the advanced

lost civilization of Atlantis. At Tiahuanaco, enormous stone blocks of more than one hundred tons can be found, one weighing an estimated 440 tons. The fact that they are strewn about the landscape hints at a tremendous geological upheaval that may have occurred some time in the distant past. It is just one of the many mysteries of this site.

Bearded White Men

Because of the lack of written records, many theories have been put forward about Tiahuanaco's origins. Early excavations of the site uncovered the remains of what appeared to be a small temple, where two large statues were found. One of these is believed to be the bearded, white-skinned god named Viracocha. Legend has it he created the Andean world and "gave rules to men how they should live, and he spoke lovingly to them with much kindness, admonishing them they should be kind to each other."[30] Similar stories about a bearded white man may be found among the legends of both the Aztecs and the Mayans. If those legends are based on fact, who were these early white men who must have visited the area long before the Spaniards? Some have suggested they were Egyptians, Cretans, Phoenicians, or Greeks because of similarities found in some designs and

The Oldest City in the World?

Until relatively recent times, it was thought that the first cities were built by the Sumerians in the Fertile Crescent area of the Middle East, between the Tigris and Euphrates rivers. Recent excavations in Palestine, however, have unearthed the remains of ancient Jericho, the oldest city yet discovered by archaeologists. Ancient Jericho, known as Tell al-Sultan, is located less than a mile from modern Jericho, approximately six miles north of the Dead Sea.

In the 1950s British archaeologist Dr. Kathleen Kenyon uncovered evidence of numerous settlements built on the same site over the centuries. The oldest ruins, at the bottom, date back to approximately 9000 B.C. Structures that have been found include the oldest known stairs, the oldest wall, and a large, round tower dating from 7000 B.C.

The ancient city of Jericho is mentioned several times in the Bible's Old Testament. The most famous story, in the sixth chapter of the Book of Joshua, tells how the walls of the city fell before the advancing Israelites. So far, archaeologists have not been able to verify the tale. As Kenyon wrote in *Digging Up Jericho*, "It is a sad fact that of the town walls of the Late Bronze Age, within which period the attack by the Israelites must fall by any dating, not a trace remains. . . . The excavation of Jericho, therefore, has thrown no light on the walls of Jericho of which the destruction is so vividly described in the Book of Joshua."

features of the architecture. No solid evidence has been found, however, to back any of these theories.

Majestic Structures

Among the structures uncovered during these early excavations were the Kalasasaya temple, the massive square archway called the Gateway of the Sun, and the remains of a large step mound known as the Akapana pyramid. Only a small part of the pyramid is still in place, as most of the stone has been carried off over the years to be used in other constructions. These structures seemed to date Tiahuanaco sometime between 400 B.C. and A.D. 100

Other ruins found approximately a mile away are truly startling. They appear to be the remains of a large wharf and a collapsed building. The building seems to be a plat-formed terraced mound like Akapana. Known as Puma Punka ("Port of the Puma"), the region was apparently once part of the shoreline of Lake Titicaca, which has receded over the centuries due to evaporation. The quarry from which the massive blocks were cut lies approximately ten miles away on the western shore of the lake. How such enormous stones could have been transported such a distance is another mystery that has stumped archaeologists.

A Controversial Theory

The ruins at Puma Punka present yet another question, since many were buried six feet below the surface. The mountain ranges in the area could not have produced sufficient water runoff to cover the ruins to such a depth, nor could wind erosion. A possible explanation is that the entire area was at one time covered by water. When it receded, it left silt that hid the ruins. This could have occurred if the city was built before the lake was even created.

If this theory has merit, one might expect to find more ruins still hidden by the lake. In November 1980 Bolivian

Pictured is a gateway to Tiahuanaco, believed to be one of the oldest cities in the world. Archaeological evidence suggests the ruins date from between 400 B.C. and A.D. 100.

author and scholar Hugo Boero Rojo announced just such a find approximately sixty feet below the surface on the northeast edge of the lake. Said Rojo:

We can now say that the existence of pre-Columbian constructions under the waters of Lake Titicaca is no longer a mere supposition or science-fiction, but a real fact. The remnants found show the existence of old civilizations that greatly antecede the Spanish colonization. We have found temples built of huge blocks of stone, with stone roads leading to unknown places and flights of steps whose bases were lost in the depths of the lake amid a thick vegetation of algae.[31]

Based in part on these findings, some archaeologists—in particular Arthur Posnansky—date the ruins back more than twelve thousand years. Posnansky backs up his theories with what is known as archaeoastronomy dating. This is based on the hypothesis that many ancient buildings were constructed by incorporating astronomical alignments with celestial bodies for religious reasons. In the case of Tiahuanaco, such alignments with the stars were in place around 15,000 B.C.

Most researchers, however, subscribe to the view that Tiahuanaco is approximately two thousand years old. Many dispute the argument that it was ever a port city on Lake Titicaca at all, believing the so-called shoreline to be nothing more than the valley wall of a river valley cut into the deposits of Lake Ballivan, on which Tiahuanaco lies. The alignments on which Posnansky based his dating, they argue, have no relevance since the ruins have been disturbed, altered, and reconstructed through the centuries. Whether the city is two thousand or twelve thousand years old is a mystery that remains to be solved.

Knossos: A City Surrounded by Myth

The Greek island of Crete in the East Mediterranean is home to the first civilization in Europe. It is believed to have been settled by the ancient Phoenicians around 7000 B.C. in the Neolithic period. Crete was the home of the Minoans, who built a seafaring empire beginning around 2000 B.C.

After approximately one thousand years, however, the civilization eventually fell victim to earthquakes and invasion. The people and their accomplishments became intertwined with myths that were passed down through the ages.

Angkor Wat

Angkor Wat is one of the most beautiful historical sites in the world. It is one of hundreds of temples in the ancient city of Angkor in the jungles of Cambodia, about 190 miles northwest of Phnom Penh. Angkor was the capital of the Khmer empire, which ruled Southeast Asia from about A.D. 880 until the beginning of the thirteenth century.

When French naturalist Henri Mouhot first came upon the ruins in 1860, he proclaimed the sandstone temple, with its graceful terraces, towers, and delicate bas-reliefs, "grander than anything left to us by Greece or Rome." Locals told him the building was the work of giants, but in reality it was constructed during the reign of Suryavarman II in the twelfth century. It was built to honor the Hindu god Vishnu, with whom the king was identified, and to eventually be used as Suryavarman's burial site. (The king's ashes may have been placed in a 213-foot-high tower in the center of the temple.)

Suryavarman left no heir when he died, and the Khmer empire went into a period of decline. People began to lose faith in their king and turned from Hinduism to Buddhism. The city finally fell to the Siamese in 1431. The invaders looted the city, planning to return the following year to finish the job. When they came back, the city that had once been home to more than a million people was deserted. By the time Mouhot rediscov-ered Angkor, the wooden palaces, public buildings, and houses had all been claimed by the jungle. All that remained were the beautiful stone-sculpted temples.

Cambodia's Angkor Wat complex was constructed in the twelfth century to honor the Hindu god Vishnu.

Theseus and the Minotaur

According to Greek mythology, Mount Ida on Crete was the site where Rhea, the Earth Mother, gave birth to Zeus, king of the gods. Zeus fathered a son named Minos, who ruled over Crete from his palace at Knossos. Minos had a son named Androgeus. He was a superb athlete and successfully represented Crete in the Athenian games. In a fit of jealousy, the king of Athens had Androgeus killed. In retaliation, Minos sent the Cretan fleet to Athens, where it conquered the city. Rather than destroy the city, however, Minos decreed that every nine years Athens would send seven young men and seven virgin women to Crete. There, Minos threw them into a labyrinth where they were sacrificed to the Minotaur, a monster with the body of a man and the head of a bull.

Theseus, the Athenian king's son, decided to put an end to the sacrifices. He volunteered to be one of the youths sent to Crete. There, he fell in love with Ariadne, King Minos's daughter. With her help, Theseus was able to slay the Minotaur.

The story had a tragic ending, however. On his way back to Athens, Theseus abandoned Ariadne on the island of Naxos. Because of a miscommunication, the Athenian king believed Theseus was dead. In despair, he threw himself into the sea and died.

The Palace at Knossos

The first attempt at separating the myths from reality was made by Minos Kalokairinos, who began excavation of the ruins at the village of Knossos on the island in 1878. It was not until Sir Arthur Evans began work at the site in 1900, however, that the wonders of this ancient civilization began to come to light. Evans started digging at a low mound on a gently sloping hillside. Over a period of thirty-one years, he eventually uncovered a huge palace, a large section of the city, and the cemeteries.

The immense palace unearthed at Knossos on the island of Crete probably served as both a cultural and a religious center for the ancient Minoan civilization.

Although no one knows if King Minos actually existed (many experts believe Minos refers to a title, such as "Pharaoh"), Evans named the civilization Minoan in his honor. The immense palace Evans uncovered occupied approximately five acres and contained fourteen hundred rooms. It likely served as a cultural and religious center as well as a capitol. Originally built around 2000 B.C., it was destroyed by earthquakes and fire and was rebuilt around 1700 B.C. and again around 1400 B.C.

Due to its massive size and complexity, some believe the palace to be the site of the labyrinth of the Minotaur legend. Others point to the depiction of bulls in Minoan artwork as hinting at the sacrifices described in the legend. Still others suggest that Theseus himself represented an army that conquered Crete.

The written language of the Minoans, known as Linear A, however, has never been deciphered. Most of what archaeologists have been able to surmise about Minoan life has come from the art, the architecture, and the artifacts that have been uncovered. Because of this, we may never know for certain where legend stops and reality begins.

Roanoke: The Lost Colony

Legend and reality are more easily separated in the case of one of the greatest mysteries in American history, the establishment of the first English settlement in the New World, the colony at Roanoke Island. The colony was established under a charter given to Sir Walter Raleigh by Queen Elizabeth, who wanted to encourage exploration of the new land. Although Raleigh organized four expeditions altogether, he himself did not make any of the trips.

The purpose of the first expedition, in 1584, was to select a suitable site for the settlement. Captains Philip Amadas and Arthur Barlowe returned to England with glowing reports about Roanoke Island, which they sighted about ten miles off the coast of present-day North Carolina. They described the island as "a most pleasant and fertile ground, replenished with goodly Cedars, and divers other sweete woods, full of Corrants [grapes], flaxe, and many other notable commodities."[32]

The following year, Raleigh sent a party of approximately 180 men on a second voyage to Roanoke Island. A colony was founded at the north end of the island, and Englishman Ralph Lane was appointed governor. Relations with the Indians were friendly at first but quickly deteriorated when a native village was burned down in retaliation for the theft of a silver cup. Supplies soon dwindled, and the settlement was eventually abandoned, with just fifteen men remaining behind.

The Second Colony

Determined to complete his mission, Raleigh recruited 117 more men, women, and children for a third trip to the New World. In July 1587 they reached Roanoke Island, where

John White, Raleigh's surveyor general on his first voyage to the new world, was appointed governor of the new "Cittie of Raleigh." Relations were reestablished with the Croatoan Indians, who informed White that some of the fifteen remaining men had been killed by an enemy tribe.

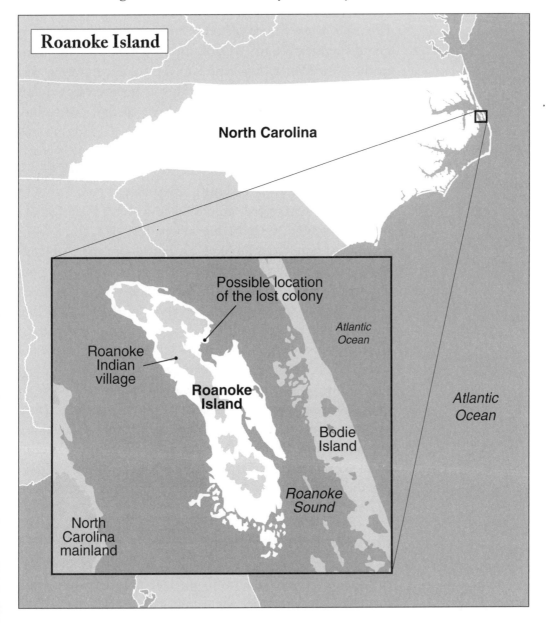

Roanoke Island

North Carolina

Possible location of the lost colony

Atlantic Ocean

Roanoke Indian village

Roanoke Island

Bodie Island

Atlantic Ocean

Roanoke Sound

North Carolina mainland

Upset at the news, White launched an attack that killed several Indians. However, White mistakenly killed the friendly Croatoans rather than the enemy tribe. Relations between the colonists and Indians deteriorated once again.

When provisions began to run low, White was forced to return to England for more supplies. Among those left at Roanoke were his daughter, Eleanor, and his newborn granddaughter, Virginia Dare, the first English child born in the New World. His return to the colony, however, was delayed for three years due to the war between Spain and England. He finally returned in 1590 to find the colony deserted and the area enclosed within a palisade of tree trunks. Into one of the trees was carved the word "CROATAN," and in another, "CRO." White believed the casings were meant "to signifie the place, where I should find the planters seated, according to a secret token agreed upon betweene them & me at my last departure from them."[33] There were no signs of battle anywhere and no bodies to be found. The ground was covered with high grass and weeds, indicating it had been abandoned for some time.

Because of the words found carved in the trees, White assumed the colony had left Roanoke Island and moved fifty miles south to Croatoan Island to live with the Indians. There was no sign, however, of the maltese cross that White and the settlers had agreed would be used as an indication they were being forced from the island. Before White could venture south, a hurricane struck, damaging the ships and forcing them back to England. Raleigh financed several expeditions that were unsuccessful in finding the settlers, and they never determined the fate of the 117 colonists.

Possible Explanations

In later years, following the establishment of the Jamestown settlement in 1607, several unsuccessful attempts were made to determine the whereabouts of the missing settlers from the Indians. Jamestown leader Captain John Smith questioned local natives and was told three similar stories. The first found the settlers attacked and massacred by Indians. Another had the Indians attack, but assimilate the women and children into the tribe. The final story had the entire colony absorbed into local tribes.

Many historians today believe the colonists went to the Croatoan village and were assimilated. Their belief is backed by reports from various sources. When English explorer John Lawson visited Roanoke Island in 1709, he visited with the Hatteras Indians, who were descendants of the Croatoans. He wrote that "several of their Ancestors were white People and could talk in a Book as we do; the Truth of which is confirmed by grey Eyes [a European, not an Indian characteristic] being found infrequently amongst these Indians, and no others."[34]

Nearly two centuries later, a North Carolina man named Hamilton MacMillan gained a great deal of attention from the academic community with his research on the Pembroke Indians of Robeson County in North Carolina. According to MacMillan, the Pembroke spoke pure Anglo-Saxon English, had light hair and an Anglo bone structure, and bore the last names of many of the lost colonists. Since no physical evidence remains, it is likely this is as close as anyone will ever get to solving the riddle of what happened to the Lost Colony of Roanoke.

Cities have disappeared from the face of the earth due to a variety of reasons. Some were destroyed by natural disasters such as earthquakes, volcanoes, floods, or prolonged drought. Others were erased by invasions or wars with neighboring societies. Still others fell into disuse over the centuries for reasons such as changes in trade routes.

Some of these once-prosperous regions have buildings or other monuments still standing to remind us of the people who once populated them. Other cities have been completely covered over by the surrounding vegetation or the

Great Zimbabwe

When sixteenth-century Portuguese explorers first came across the ruins of Great Zimbabwe, they believed they had found the legendary mines of King Solomon. Covering nearly eighteen hundred acres, the ruins were comprised of three main groupings: the Hill Complex, the Valley Complex, and the Great Enclosure. As reported by historian João de Barros, Arab traders described the largest of the structures as "a square fortress of masonry within and without, built of stones of marvellous size, and there appears to be no mortar joining them." This outer wall of the Great Enclosure is 820 feet around and thirty-six feet high. Enclosed within are several stone structures, including the mysterious Conical Tower. This monument is thirty-three feet tall, with a base sixteen feet in diameter. It is solid, with no windows or doors, and composed of granite blocks throughout. Its purpose is a mystery, but it is believed to have been some sort of religious symbol.

In a region of Africa where mud huts were the norm, this city of stone located to the east of the Kalahari Desert between the Zambezi and Limpopo rivers in Rhodesia (present-day Zimbabwe) looked curiously out of place. Later travelers, such as German geologist Karl Mauch, attributed the construction to the Egyptians or Phoenicians, unable to accept that such work could possibly be a product of African origin.

Modern archaelogists now believe the structures are the ruins of a town built between A.D. 1200 and A.D. 1450. At one time it probably had a population between ten thousand and eighteen thousand. It was not until 1932 that it was proved to be of African origin. Questions remain, however, about how it was constructed and why the civilization that built it declined. Since the inhabitants of Great Zimbabwe left behind no written records, it is likely that these questions will never be answered.

A massive outer wall encircles the Great Enclosure of the Great Zimbabwe complex.

accumulation of centuries of dust and dirt. Many of these ancient communities have only recently begun revealing their secrets to researchers who sift through their ruins. As archaeologists dig deeper and deeper, more and more of the wonders of our distant forefathers are revealed. Through these revelations, we also learn more and more about ourselves.

Chapter 4

Pyramids and Burial Grounds

Some of the most magnificent monuments built by man were constructed to honor their gods and kings, who sometimes were believed to be the gods' representatives on earth. These larger-than-life figures were worshipped both in life and after death. Their worshippers often went to extraordinary lengths to assure that these king-gods would enjoy the afterlife as much as possible.

Many of these tombs are surrounded in mystery. Some appear to be reaching up to the heavens themselves, so immense in stature that their construction must have required years of toil by thousands of workers. Can such gargantuan works have been undertaken solely to house the remains of a single person, or was there another reason for their construction? How could some of these monuments have been built to such a degree of precision using only the most primitive measuring devices? Many ancient legends suggest that such works could only have been constructed with the help of the gods themselves. Is it possible these so-called gods were really extraterrestrial visitors from another world in a distant galaxy?

Ancient Wonders

The ancient world is known for many magnificent structures. Seven of these—the Hanging Gardens of Babylon, the Temple of Artemis at Ephesus, the Statue of Zeus at Olympia, the Lighthouse of Alexandria, the Colossus of Rhodes, the Mausoleum at Halicarnassus, and the Great Pyramid of Giza—are remembered collectively as the Seven Wonders of the Ancient World. Today, some four and a half thousand years after its creation, the Great Pyramid is the only one that remains standing.

That magnificent monument is the most striking example of pyramid building that occurred in what is known as

The Great Pyramid at Giza, Egypt, is one of the Seven Wonders of the Ancient World. The pharaoh Cheops built this pyramid to rival all other pyramids.

the Old Kingdom (2686 B.C. to 2181 B.C.), sometimes referred to as the Pyramid Age. Some ninety such structures from that era have survived to the present day in some form.

The Afterlife

The people who lived during the time of the pyramids believed their kings, known as pharaohs (originally meaning "great house"), were gods. The ancient Egyptians believed that death was the beginning of a journey into the afterlife. The deceased king became Osiris, the king of the dead. The pharaoh who replaced him became Horus, god of the heavens and protector of the sun god. A part of the dead king's spirit, called the *ka*, was believed to remain with the body. If it was not protected, it wold not be able to perform its otherworldly duties. The result could be disaster for the country.

In an effort to avoid such a catastrophe, the dead king's body was mummified, or preserved. All the possessions he might need in the afterlife were buried with him. In order to protect and preserve the *ka* that remained with the body, a tomb was built. These tombs were often cut into the bedrock and covered with a flat-roofed structure called a mastaba. These, in turn, were sometimes covered with mounds of dirt. It is possible that the shape of the later pyramid tombs might have been derived from these mounds. It is therefore possible to think of a pyramid, wrote authors Kevin Jackson and Jonathan Stamp, as "a machine for turning a king into a god."[35]

The First Pyramid

The first pyramid was built by Pharaoh Djoser. It began as a flat-roofed mastaba, but eventually had six layers, or steps, added to it. By the end of Djoser's reign in 2611 B.C., the pyramid stood 204 feet high. Rather than being constructed of mud brick as its predecessors, much of Djoser's

Step Pyramid at Saqqara consisted of harder, more durable stone. Many historians attribute this "invention" to Djoser's chief architect, Imhotep.

In addition to the underground burial chamber, the Step Pyramid also contains three and a half miles of tunnels, shafts, stairwells, and passages built to confuse and hinder potential grave robbers. The pyramid itself was part of a complex that included temples, courtyards, and chapels, covering an area of nearly forty acres. The entire compound was enclosed by a thirty-foot-high wall. Imhotep's design provided the model from which all subsequent pyramid complexes were developed.

A Prolific Builder

Arguably the greatest pyramid builder of all was the pharaoh Sneferu, who came into power in 2575 B.C. Sneferu was responsible for the construction of several important monuments. The first began as a step pyramid at Meidum. Fifteen years later, Sneferu apparently changed his mind and sent workers back to fill in the original steps to form the smooth-surfaced structure we generally think of as a pyramid today. His was also the first pyramid to have an aboveground burial chamber. Because of its current ruined state, there is no way of knowing for certain if what became known as Sneferu Endures was ever actually completed.

Between the time construction on this first pyramid was begun and the time it was completed, Sneferu built two other monuments at Dahshur, north of Meidum. One, called the Southern Shining Pyramid, is better known today as the Bent Pyramid. It got this name due to the fact that the slope of the sides becomes less steep approximately halfway to the top. It is theorized that the change may have been made because the steeper slope would have made the pyramid unstable.

The imperfections of the Bent Pyramid are likely what prompted Sneferu to start construction on another project

at Dahshur. Originally called the Shining Pyramid, it is now known as the North or Red Pyramid and was the first successful, true cased pyramid (one with a layer of casing stone covering its outer surface) in Egypt. Most of its core was constructed of reddish limestone, with finer white limestone used as a casing stone. At 345 feet tall, it is the fourth-tallest pyramid ever built in Egypt, and it was completed in approximately seventeen years.

The Great Pyramid

When Sneferu died, he was succeeded by his third son, Prince Khufu (also known as Cheops). Facing the challenge of outdoing his father's pyramid-building achievements, Khufu moved the royal necropolis (literally, "city of the dead") to the Giza Plateau, just north of modern-day Cairo. It was selected for its closeness to the Nile River (so that building materials could be easily transported) and to the Egyptian capital city of Memphis, and for its geological appeal (a plain was necessary in order to construct a level foundation).

The first step in constructing the pyramid was laying a flat foundation. This was accomplished with an astonishing degree of accuracy, as the immense structure is level to within less than an inch. Although it is not known for certain, it is believed that this accuracy was achieved through the use of water, possibly by building a shallow wall of mud, filling it with water, then cutting a series of trenches the same distance beneath the water's surface. After the water was drained, the area between the trenches was carved until the rock was perfectly flat.

In addition to being leveled, the foundation also had to be aligned precisely with the north, the south, the east, and

The Great Pyramid rests almost perfectly level on a flat foundation, and it is precisely aligned with the cardinal points of the compass.

the west. Using an instrument called a *merkhet*, this was somehow accomplished to an impressive degree of accuracy. The most precisely aligned of all the pyramids, the Great Pyramid deviates from true north by little more than an average of three minutes of one degree (there are sixty minutes in one degree). How the Egyptians were able to achieve this level of precision with such primitive tools is one of the most intriguing questions associated with the construction.

The Workforce

Rather than having been constructed by slaves, as was believed for many years, the pyramid at Giza was built by an army of laborers. This army was also much smaller than originally suspected. The Greek historian Herodotus asserted that one hundred thousand men were needed to cut, move, and set the 2.3 million stones—each with an average weight of two and a half tons—that went into the construction of the Great Pyramid. It has now been established, however, that the entire job could have been done by a workforce of as few as thirty-three hundred men working at any one time. Modern Egyptologists believe the actual number of laborers involved to be somewhere around twenty thousand.

The workers cut the stones from what is known as the Khufu Quarry, about one thousand feet south of the pyramid, and from other quarries east of the Nile. They were transported by barge, then dragged to the site. After the stones of the first level were set, others were dragged up to each succeeding level on a series of ramps. A capstone, or *pyramidion*, was the last section to be placed at the very top.

Once the pyramid was completed, workers turned their attention to the completion of the other elements of the necropolis. These included several smaller satellite pyramids, a mortuary temple, a valley temple, a great stone causeway, and more.

Inside the Great Pyramid

The interior of the Great Pyramid is divided into three main areas: the Subterranean Chamber; the Queen's Chamber; and the Grand Gallery and King's Burial Chamber. The Subterranean Chamber is below the bedrock of the Giza Plateau. It is reached by a long passageway that extends down from the entrance, about fifty-five feet above ground level on the north face. This chamber was never completed, and its purpose remains a mystery.

From the Subterranean Chamber, the Queen's Chamber (a misleading name given by early explorers) is reached by going back up the descending passage to a point where it intersects with an ascending passage. Rather than being a burial chamber, the room is believed to be a *serdab*, or room containing a large statue representing the king's *ka*, or "life force." In the event the royal body came to harm in the afterlife, the *ka* statue could replace it.

The Grand Gallery is basically a continuation of the ascending passageway. It eventually leads to an antechamber from which the King's Burial Chamber can be reached. This large room contains a lidless sarcophagus, or tomb. Two narrow diagonal shafts lead upward and outward to the pyramid's exterior face, one oriented toward the North Pole Star and the other to the constellation of Orion.

Pyramid Speculations

The construction of the Great Pyramid gives rise to several questions. If it was indeed built as a tomb, why have no symbols or possessions of royalty—much less the corpse of the king—ever been found? When it was explored for the first time in the ninth century by Arab caliph Abdullah al-Mamun, the group that entered the tomb found the ascending passageway blocked by several large granite plugs. These had obviously been placed during the pyramid's construction so that the inner chamber would not be disturbed by robbers and looters. The Arabs were able to

The Great Sphinx

Located not far from the three pyramids on the Giza Plateau is the Great Sphinx, another one of Egypt's many mysterious monuments. The Sphinx is a creature with the body of a lion and the head of a human being. Its name is derived from the Greek word *sphingo*, meaning "to strangle." This comes from the Greek Sphinx's habit of strangling its victims.

The Great Sphinx is believed to have been constructed around 2540 B.C. by the pharaoh Khafre. It is 241 feet long and 65 feet high. Between its forelegs is a stela, or inscribed slab, placed there by Thutmose IV approximately one thousand years after the monument's construction. It recounts Thutmose's dream that the Sphinx promised him kingship if he would clear the sand from around the figure's body. (The body was buried in sand for most of its existence.) Thutmose eventually completed the task shortly after ascending to the throne.

Rather than being carved from a single rock, the body of the Great Sphinx was formed from huge blocks of soft limestone. The head was sculpted from harder limestone, with separate blocks for the forelegs. Over the centuries, much of the figure has eroded due to the ravages of the wind and sand. Planned restorations have not been as successful as hoped, and they continue to the present day.

It is entirely possible there are yet-to-be-discovered chambers around or under the Sphinx. Evidence of such hollow spaces exists, but no further examination of them has been allowed. Questions of what these chambers might contain were fueled by American psychic Edgar Cayce in the 1940s. While in a trance, Cayce predicted they would contain records originating with the survivors from the lost continent of Atlantis. Others suggest it was built to guard the king's tomb, located in one of the neighboring pyramids.

Constructed around 2540 B.C., the Great Sphinx is comprised of several individual blocks of carved limestone.

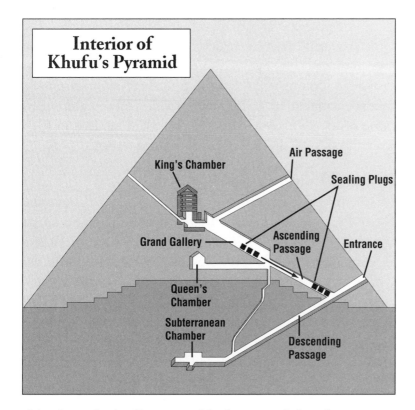

Interior of Khufu's Pyramid

King's Chamber

Air Passage

Sealing Plugs

Grand Gallery

Ascending Passage

Entrance

Queen's Chamber

Subterranean Chamber

Descending Passage

chip through the limestone blocks around the plugs, eventually making their way to the King's Burial Chamber, where they found the empty sarcophagus. If looters had indeed beaten them to the tomb, how had they managed to get past the plugs?

Others doubt such an enormous structure could have been constructed by people using primitive tools and instruments. One theory suggests an advanced civilization that inhabited the lost continent of Atlantis is responsible. Other alternative explanations tend to be even more imaginative. Says astrophysicist and UFO buff Morris K. Jessup, "Levitation is the only feasible answer. I believe that this lifting machine was a spaceship, probably of vast proportions; that it brought colonists to various parts of the earth . . . that it supplied the heavy lift power for erecting great stone works; and that it was suddenly destroyed or taken away."[36]

Some people doubt that such a massive structure as the Great Pyramid was constructed solely to shelter a single royal mummy. The pyramid's near-perfect north-south and east-west alignment has led some to theorize it was also a sundial, a calendar, and an astronomical observatory. Because of its placement, shadows cast could be used to keep track of hours of the day and seasons of the year.

Pyramid Power

In recent years, new theories have arisen, not about the Great Pyramid itself, but rather about the pyramid shape and the unusual effects it may have on objects. In 1920 a Frenchman named Antoine Bovis toured the King's Burial Chamber and reported finding the remains of several small animals that had apparently died there. Their dehydrated bodies surprisingly had no odor. Bovis returned home to France where he experimented with a small pyramid he made out of wood. He placed several objects inside it, including a dead cat, some meat, and a few eggs. In each case, according to Bovis, the organic matter dried out and mummified rather than decayed. His experiments were duplicated by a Czech radio engineer named Karl Drbal. Drbal also placed a razor blade inside his model of a miniature pyramid and claimed that the blade was somehow regenerated and made sharper than it had been before.

Although scientists have failed to replicate these fanciful results, there remain those who believe the Great Pyramid still has many secrets to reveal. As William Fix, author of *Pyramid Odyssey*, asserts, "It is enormous; it is ancient; it is legendary; it is sophisticated; it is the result of great enterprise; it is here for all to see at the crossroads of the earth—and it does not seem to belong to our world."[37]

Pyramids in the Americas

The magnificent structures in Egypt are the first that come to mind when the word *pyramid* is heard, but there are actually many more located in the tropical forests of the Americas. Some archaeologists estimate that Mexico alone might be home to as many as one hundred thousand pyramids that are hidden by vegetation and have not yet been uncovered.

These pre-Columbian pyramids have little in common with their Egyptian counterparts. Rather than being smooth-sided structures that reach a summit, the pyramids of Middle America were generally built in a series of tiers, culminating in a flat top on which was situated a small temple. The temple allowed the priests to be nearer to the heavens and their gods. The pyramid's main purpose was to be a base for the temple, not a tomb for a king, as in Egypt. The pyramids usually had steps so the priests—and those intended for sacrifice—were able to ascend to the top.

The pre-Columbian pyramid of the Americas was built to accommodate a temple at its summit. The temple's location atop the pyramid allowed priests to be closer to the gods.

Teotihuacán

The origins of Mesoamerican (Mexican–Central American) civilization are shrouded in mystery. The earliest well-defined state was that of the Olmecs, who flourished from around 1500 B.C. to 500 B.C. in the Vera Cruz region of Mexico. They were responsible for the first pyramid mounds in the area.

By the time of Christ, Teotihuacán had arisen as an important urban center, lying about thirty miles northeast of present-day Mexico City. (The name *Teotihuacán*, meaning "City of the Gods," is attributed to the Aztecs, who settled there in about A.D. 1500. It is not known what the inhabitants themselves called the city.) It was not long until it developed into the largest settlement in the Americas, with a population of more than one hundred thousand. It was also home to some six hundred pyramids.

Today, centuries after its abandonment, questions remain to be answered. Who were the people of Teotihuacán, and where did they come from? What was the reason for the city's rapid decline and eventual destruction? Where did the inhabitants go, and why?

The Pyramid of the Moon and the Pyramid of the Sun

The city of Teotihuacán was laid out in a vast geometrical arrangement, built to a remarkably precise grid pattern. The main street of the city was the Avenue of the Dead, so named because the mounds along the sides were at one time believed to be tombs. (Most were actually pyramid-shaped apartment compounds.) At the extreme north end of this three-mile-long thoroughfare stands the Pyramid of the Moon. This magnificent structure is actually seven buildings on top of one another. Each time the building was modified, the old one was covered with dirt and stones and refaced with stone sculpture. Recent excavations have uncovered a previously unknown tomb containing jade artifacts, which appear to be Mayan in style.

The Pyramid of the Sun (background) located at the eastern end of Teotihuacán's Avenue of the Dead is one of the tallest pyramids in the world.

Less than a mile to the south of the Pyramid of the Moon, on the east side of the Avenue of the Dead, lies the city's largest pyramid. Towering high above the surrounding plateau is the enormous Pyramid of the Sun. The temple that once graced its summit is long gone, but at 216 feet high, it is still one of the tallest pyramids in the world. The magnificent structure rises into the sky from a base whose sides measure more than two football fields in length. Probably completed in the first century A.D., archaeologists estimate it took at least fifty years to finish, with a workforce of thousands. About 1 million cubic yards of material were used in its construction.

The Feathered Serpent Pyramid

Located in the geographic center of Teotihuacán is a huge, enclosed temple called the Ciudadela (Citadel). Measuring about thirteen hundred feet on each side, it is composed of an interior space surrounded by four large platforms topped by pyramids. The Feathered Serpent Pyramid is the central pyramid of the complex.

Although only third in size to the Sun and Moon pyramids, the Feathered Serpent Pyramid, honoring the god Quetzalcóatl, is much more elaborate. The four sides of the six-stepped structure are covered by an ornate facade of stone carvings, including many large sculpted heads. The structure also includes a grave complex in which the remains of more than one hundred individuals have been recovered. It is believed the majority of the victims were soldiers who were sacrificed.

End of an Empire

Soldiers may also have played a part in Teotihuacán's eventual destruction. Many believe the city was invaded and destroyed by nomadic warrior tribes from the north. Other evidence seems to point to a series of large-scale fires causing widespread damage. No one knows for sure,

The Palenque Astronaut

In the foothills of the Tumbalá mountains of Chiapas, Mexico, lie the ruins of the ancient Mayan site of Palenque. One of the most notable structures at Palenque is the pyramid known as the Temple of Inscriptions. When Alberto Ruz examined the site in 1948, he came across a secret passage filled with rubble. It was not until four years later that the rubble was cleared away to reveal the tomb of King Pacal. It also revealed a mystery that has been a source of controversy to the present day.

Covering the sarcophagus (tomb) is a massive stone lid with a detailed relief of the figure of a man. According to Mayan legend, the relief depicts the descent of King Pacal into the underworld. Soviet scientist Alexander Kazantev, however, proposed the theory that the figure was actually an astronaut and his spaceship. The theory was popularized in the late 1960s by Erich von Däniken in his book *Chariots of the Gods?* According to von Däniken:

There sits a human being, with the upper part of his body bent forward like a racing motorcyclist; today any child would identify his vehicle as a rocket. It is pointed at the front, then changes to strangely grooved indenta-

tions like inlet ports, widens out, and terminates at the tail in a darting flame. The crouching being himself is manipulating a number of indefinable controls and has the heel of his left foot on a kind of pedal. . . . Our space traveler . . . is not only bent forward tensely; he is also looking intently at an apparatus hanging in front of his face. The astronaut's front seat is separated by struts from the rear portion of the vehicle, in which symmetrically arranged boxes, circles, points, and spirals can be seen.

If von Däniken is correct, then the Mayans were visited by extraterrestrials more than a thousand years ago.

Some believe that the lid covering a sarcophagus found in the Temple of Inscriptions (pictured) depicts an extraterrestrial and his spaceship.

and the city's demise remains shrouded in mystery. Long after its fall, however, Teotihuacán's influence on Mesoamerican civilization continued to be felt. With only about 10 percent of the ancient metropolis having been excavated, perhaps future work will unlock more of the city's mysteries.

The Pyramids of China

When mysteries are discussed, the pyramids of China must be right near the top of the list. Until relatively recent times, the outside world had virtually no knowledge of these earth pyramids scattered throughout various regions of the country. A grainy black-and-white photograph taken by a U.S. Air Force pilot at the end of World War II is the first evidence we have that such structures exist. Although that famous White Pyramid is rumored to be as much as one thousand feet tall (more than twice the height of the Great Pyramid), most of the Chinese pyramids, built of mud and dirt, are much smaller.

In 1994 German researcher and author Hartwig Hausdorf was able to visit the "forbidden zones" surrounding the city of Xi'an, the capital of Shaanxi province in central China. There, he found and photographed several of these pyramids. He estimated there were more than one hundred such earth mounds in the region. One of these is Mount Li, the fifteen-story-tall burial mound of Qin Shi Huang, the first emperor of China and the builder of the Great Wall.

Qin inherited the throne of the kingdom in 246 B.C. when he was just thirteen years old. Over the next twenty-five years, he ruled with a ruthless hand and unified all of China. He also began work on an imperial tomb to be his eternal home after his death. Construction of the complex was a mammoth undertaking, as described by early historian Ssu-ma Ch'ien about 100 B.C.:

> As soon as the First Emperor became king of Ch'in, excavations and building had been started at Mount

Li, while after he won the empire, more than 700,000 conscripts from all parts of the country worked there. They dug through three subterranean streams and poured molten copper for the outer coffin, and the tomb was filled with models of palaces, pavilions, and offices, as well as fine vessels, precious stones, and rarities. Artisans were ordered to fix up crossbows so that any thief breaking in would be shot. All the country's streams, the Yellow River, and the Yangtze were reproduced in quicksilver and by some mechanical means made to flow into a miniature ocean. The heavenly constellations were above and the regions of the earth below. The candles were made of whale oil to ensure their burning for the longest possible time.[38]

Physical evidence of the construction, however, would not come to light until hundreds of years later.

An Incredible Discovery

Although the earth mound that covers the emperor's final resting place had long been recognized by archaeologists, the extent of the ancient burial site was not imagined until 1974. In the spring of that year, some peasant farmers made an incredible discovery while digging a well less than a mile from the mound. They uncovered some pottery which led to the uncovering of a huge subterranean vault that was part of the immense grave complex. Further excavations have revealed it to be the greatest archaeological discovery of recent times.

So far, three large pits have been found on the three-acre site. Within them, an army of an estimated eight thousand terra-cotta armed warriors, servants, and horses stand guard, together with assorted other treasures. Many of the figures are broken and scattered about, victims of soldiers who burned and looted a part of the site after Qin's death.

The statues, buried in a huge roofed gallery, were intended to guard the emperor's tomb. The figures carried real weapons, and the horses pulled real chariots. Around 1500 B.C. live servants and warriors were occasionally buried with early kings. By entombing the clay statues, Qin revived the practice symbolically.

The Terra-Cotta Warriors

The first pit to be uncovered contained approximately six thousand figures, in a rectangular formation of chariots and army troops. The second pit, excavated two years later, contained about fourteen hundred warriors and horses, and sixty-four chariots in a winding formation. The third—and smallest—pit appeared to be a command headquarters, with six warriors, one chariot, and some weapons. It is believed several dozen more pits might still lie hidden.

Ziggurats

A type of structure similar to the pyramid is the ziggurat, which was popular among the Sumerians, the Babylonians, and the Assyrians. These people built temples to their gods atop enormous towers that consisted of a series of platforms (numbering from two to seven), each decreasing in size as they climbed. Some rose as high as three hundred feet. The core of the ziggurat was composed of sun-baked bricks, while the facings were made of fired bricks glazed with different colors. The shrine at the top was reached by a series of stairs on one side, or a spiral ramp that ran from base to summit.

The most famous of these structures was the ziggurat of Etemenanki, believed to be the biblical Tower of Babel. Standing near the Euphrates River in Babylon, this magnificent building has long since been reduced to rubble, with only the outline of its enormous square base remaining. About twenty-five ziggurats still remain today, with the best preserved being the ziggurat of Ur-Nammu in present-day Iraq, and the largest, that of Tchoga Zanbil in Iran.

At one time, it was believed that ziggurats might have concealed tombs like the pyramids. Today, most archaeologists believe they were built as pedestals from which the gods could come down to bestow blessings on their followers. In this way, the tower acted as a kind of bridge between heaven and earth, allowing the gods to become closer to mankind.

Rather than being identical, each of the figures is approximately six feet tall with its own distinct features. As archaeologist Ch'en Hsuch-hue explained, "We believe this is because the emperor ordered the artists to model realistic portraits of each warrior, servant, and footman in his live honor guard, so they could continue to guard him after death."[39]

An Impressive Undertaking

Perhaps the most puzzling mystery surrounding the terra-cotta warriors concerns their construction. Based on three years of study, most archaeologists have concluded that they were fired in kilns relatively close to Qin's tomb. How so many were produced is a bigger mystery.

The clay that was used was panned and crushed into a form suitable for molding. The figure was then started from the bottom of the body. Coils of wet clay formed the body and arms, with the clay smoothed by using a paddle. (Paddle marks found inside broken statues confirm this procedure.)

Molds were used to mass-produce hands, heads, and ears. Details of the face and armor were crafted manually. After smearing the surface of the head with a fine clay, facial details were formed by pinching, carving, cutting, and pasting. No two faces are the same. The completed figures were then transported to nearby kilns for firing. After hardening, several layers of gelatin and lacquer were applied to each statue to add color. Despite many attempts, modern craftsmen have not been able to create figures of similar quality. Reported Professor Gao Zhengyao at Zhengzhou University in China's Henan province, "It is hard to imagine how so many terra-cotta warriors and horses were made during the very brief dynasty, which existed 2000 years ago, as it would take months to duplicate one by modern means."[40]

The terra-cotta warriors were enclosed in a roofed area measuring seven hundred feet by two hundred feet. Most

The Chinese emperor Qin Shi Huang had these lifelike terra-cotta warriors entombed with him as a form of protection in the afterlife.

were buried standing erect, in battle formation, just as the emperor's troops would have been when going into battle. The horses were placed four across in front of the chariots.

In addition to the soldiers, horses, and chariots, numerous other pieces were interred. These include linen, pottery, utensils, iron tools, and bronze objects, as well as artifacts of gold, jade, bamboo, and bone. Perhaps these will help unlock more of the secrets behind the terra-cotta warriors of China. Even if they do, however, there will always be other sites waiting to take their place on the long list of the world's most mysterious places.

Most societies honor their dead in one way or another. Few, however, have done so in the manner of those who constructed pyramids and temples in their honor. Years of work went into the construction of these buildings, whose beauty and majesty continue to amaze us. The fact that such deeds were done without the miracles of modern technology is hard to fathom. It serves to remind us of humanity's unlimited capacity and potential.

Notes

Chapter One: Stone Sentinels

1. Quoted in Editors of Time-Life Books, *Mystic Places*. Alexandria, VA: Time-Life Books, 1987, p. 82.
2. Quoted in *Mystic Places*, p. 84.
3. Robert Wernick and Editors of Time-Life Books, *The Monument Builders*. New York: Time-Life Books, 1973, p. 112.
4. Quoted in David Souden, *Stonehenge Revealed*. New York: Facts On File, 1997, p. 89.
5. Quoted in Sandra Dimitrakopoulos, "Stonehenge: Unearthing a Mystery," *Discovery Channel Canada*, October 12, 1999. www.exn.ca.
6. Quoted in Sandra Dimitrakopoulos, "Mystery of Stonehenge Points to the Heavens," *Discovery Channel Canada*, October 12, 1999. www.exn.ca.
7. Quoted in Harold D. Edgerton, "Stonehenge," *National Geographic*, June 1960, p. 863.
8. Quoted in Anne-Elisabeth Riskine, "Carnac, the Army of Stones (Morbihan)," *Ministry of Culture and Communication*. www.culture.fr.
9. Quoted in Editors of Time-Life Books, *Mysterious Lands and Peoples*. Alexandria, VA: Time-Life Books, 1991, p. 84.
10. Quoted in David Wallechinsky and Irving Wallace, *The People's Almanac*. Garden City, NY: Doubleday, 1975, p. 1,377.

Chapter Two: Earth Etchings

11. Quoted in Gloria Chang, "Peruvian Desert: A Perfect Tableau for Nazcan 'Artists,'" *Discovery Channel Canada*, October 12, 1999. www.exn.ca.
12. Quoted in Loren McIntyre, "Mystery of the Ancient Nazca Lines," *National Geographic*, May 1975, p. 720.
13. Quoted in Reader's Digest, *The World's Last Mysteries*. Pleasantville, NY: Reader's Digest Association, 1978, p. 282.
14. Quoted in Evan Hadingham, *Lines to the Mountain Gods*. New York: Random House, 1987, p. 70.
15. Quoted in McIntyre, "Mystery of the Ancient Nazca Lines," p. 725.
16. Quoted in McIntyre, "Mystery of the Ancient Nazca Lines," p. 718.
17. Quoted in Hadingham, *Lines to the Mountain Gods*, p. 42.
18. Quoted in McIntyre, "Mystery of the Ancient Nazca Lines," p. 725.
19. Quoted in Freddy Silva, "Crop Circles: The Formative Years, "*Crop Circular*. www.lovely.clara.net.
20. Quoted in Joe Nickell, "Levengood's Crop-Circle Plant Research," *Skeptical Briefs*, vol. 6, no. 2, June 1996. www.csicop.org.

21. Donna Yavelak, "Crop Circles: A Deeper Look," *Foundation for Paranormal Research*. www.paranormal researchonline.com.

22. Freddy Silva, "So It's All Done with Planks and Bits of String, Is It?" *The Crop Circular*. www.lovely.clara. net.

23. Quoted in Stephen Wagner, "Crop Circles: Best Evidence," *About*. http:// paranormal.about.com.

24. Quoted in *Wiltshire White Horses*, "The Uffington White Horse." http://wiltshire whitehorses.org.uk.

Chapter Three:
Lost and Abandoned Cities

25. Quoted in Reader's Digest, *The World's Last Mysteries*, p. 160.

26. Quoted in Reader's Digest, *The World's Last Mysteries*, p. 161.

27. Hiram Bingham, *Lost City of the Incas*. New York: Atheneum, 1969, p. 182.

28. Quoted in Andy Carvin, "Machu Picchu: Jewel of the Andes," *EdWeb*. www.edwebproject.org.

29. Quoted in Reader's Digest, *The World's Last Mysteries*. p. 133.

30. Quoted in *Museum of Unnatural History*, "Lost Cities." www.unmuseum.org.

31. Quoted in Helmut Zetti, "Tiahuanaco and the Deluge," *Catastrophism and Ancient History*, vol. VI, part 2, July

1984. www.thule.org.

32. Quoted in Charles W. Porter III, *Fort Raleigh National Historic Site North Carolina*. Washington, DC: National Park Service Historical Handbook Series, no. 16, 1965.

33. Quoted in David Stick, *Roanoke Island: The Beginnings of English America*. Chapel Hill: University of North Carolina Press, 1983.

34. Quoted in Kenneth B. Platnick, *Great Mysteries of History*. New York: Harper & Row, 1971, p. 90.

Chapter Four:
Pyramids and Burial Grounds

35. Kevin Jackson and Jonathan Stamp, *Building the Great Pyramid*. Toronto: Firefly Books, 2003, p. 108.

36. Quoted in Wallechinsky and Wallace, *The People's Almanac*, p. 1,364.

37. Quoted in Editors of Time-Life Books, *Mystic Places*, p. 82.

38. Quoted in Audrey Toppin, "China's Incredible Find," *National Geographic*, April 1978, p. 448.

39. Quoted in Toppin, "China's Incredible Find," p. 448.

40. Quoted in *People's Daily*, "China Reveals First Clue in Riddle of Terracotta Warriors," November 23, 2002. www.english.peopledaily.com.cn.

For Further Reading

Paul Bahn and John Flenley, *Easter Island, Earth Island.* New York: Thames and Hudson, 1992. The complete story of the Easter Island statues and the people who constructed them.

Christopher Chippindale, *Stonehenge Complete.* New York: Thames and Hudson, 1994. An ideal introduction to the most famous and mysterious of all Europe's ancient sites.

Daniel Cohen, *Hiram Bingham and the Dream of Gold.* New York: M. Evans, 1984. The fascinating adventures of Hiram Bingham, who made the greatest archaeological find of the century, the rediscovery of Machu Picchu.

Lee Miller, *Roanoke: Solving the Mystery of the Lost Colony.* New York: Penguin Books, 2000. A new investigation into America's oldest unsolved mystery.

Jennifer Westwood, ed., *The Atlas of Mysterious Places: The World's Unexplained Sacred Sites, Symbolic Landscapes, Ancient Cities, and Lost Lands.* New York: Grove Press, 1987. This volume contains many beautiful pictures of the world's mysterious places.

Works Consulted

Books

Hiram Bingham, *Lost City of the Incas.* New York: Atheneum, 1969. Hiram Bingham's own story of the discovery of Machu Picchu, the Lost City of the Incas.

Erich von Däniken, *Chariots of the Gods?* New York; Bantam Books, 1968. This best-selling book introduced the theory that ancient earth had been visited by aliens.

Editors of Time-Life Books, *Mysterious Lands and Peoples.* Alexandria, VA: Time-Life Books, 1991. This volume in the Mysteries of the Unknown series contains a chapter—"Enigmas of the Islands"—that delves into the mysteries of the islands of the South Pacific, including Easter Island.

————, *Mystic Places.* Alexandria, VA: Time-Life Books, 1987. This volume in the Mysteries of the Unknown series contains chapters on "Secrets of the Great Pyramid," the "Meaning of the Megaliths," and "Pictures on the Earth."

D. Garnett, ed., *The Letters of T.E. Lawrence.* London: Spring Books, 1964. A revised edition of the collected letters of the famous explorer.

Evan Hadingham, *Lines to the Mountain Gods.* New York: Random House, 1987. A thorough examination of the Nazca lines, their designers, and their possible purposes.

Kevin Jackson and Jonathan Stamp, *Building the Great Pyramid.* Toronto: Firefly Books, 2003. This volume traces the history of the Great Pyramid and also examines the origins of Egyptology.

Kathleen M. Kenyon, *Digging Up Jericho.* London: Ernest Benn, 1957. The story of the excavations at the site of the biblical city.

Kenneth B. Platnick, *Great Mysteries of History.* New York: Harper & Row, 1971. A look at sixteen of history's mysteries, including the Lost Colony of Roanoke and Stonehenge.

Charles W. Porter III, *Fort Raleigh National Historic Site North Carolina.* Washington, DC: National Park Service Historical Handbook Series, no. 16, 1965. One of a series of handbooks describing the historical and archaeological areas in the National Park Service system.

Reader's Digest, *The World's Last Mysteries.* Pleasantville, NY: Reader's Digest

Association, 1978. This 320-page, lavishly illustrated volume examines many of the world's great mysteries.

David Souden, *Stonehenge Revealed*. New York: Facts On File, 1997. This beautifully illustrated volume details the fascinating story of Stonehenge.

David Stick, *Roanoke Island: The Beginnings of English America*. Chapel Hill: University of North Carolina Press, 1983. The fascinating story from North Carolina's past, from the first expedition sent out by Sir Walter Raleigh in 1584 to the mysterious disappearance of what has become known as the Lost Colony of Roanoke.

David Wallechinsky and Irving Wallace, *The People's Almanac*. Garden City, NY: Doubleday, 1975. "The first reference book ever prepared to be read for pleasure" features over twenty-five thousand entries, including a chapter on "The Unknown and Mysterious."

Simon Welfare and John Fairley, *Arthur C. Clarke's Mysterious World*. New York: A & W, 1980. A compendium of strange events and unexplained phenomena based on the thirteen-part television series of the same name.

Robert Wernick and Editors of Time-Life Books, *The Monument Builders*. New York: Time-Life Books, 1973. This volume in The Emergence of Man series takes a look at the megaliths of western Europe and their builders, with emphasis on the construction of Stonehenge.

Periodicals

Harold D. Edgerton, "Stonehenge," *National Geographic*, June 1960.

Loren McIntyre, "Mystery of the Ancient Nazca Lines," *National Geographic*, May 1975.

Audrey Toppin, "China's Incredible Find," *National Geographic*, April 1978.

Internet Sources

Andy Carvin, "Machu Picchu: Jewel of the Andes," *EdWeb*. www.edwebproject.org.

Gloria Chang, "Peruvian Desert: A Perfect Tableau for Nazcan 'Artists,'" *Discovery Channel Canada*, October 12, 1999. www.exn.ca.

Sandra Dimitrakopoulos, "Mystery of Stonehenge Points to the Heavens," *Discovery Channel Canada*, October 12, 1999. www.exn.ca.

———, "Stonehenge: Unearthing a Mystery," *Discovery Channel Canada*, October 12, 1999. www.exn.ca.

Museum of Unnatural History, "Lost Cities." www.unmuseum.org.

Joe Nickell, "Levengood's Crop-Circle Plant Research," *Skeptical Briefs*, vol. 6, no. 2, June 1996. www.csicop.org.

People's Daily, "China Reveals First Clue in Riddle of Terra-cotta Warriors,"

November 23, 2002. www.english.people daily.com.cn.

Anne-Elisabeth Riskine, "Carnac, the Army of Stones (Morbihan)," *Ministry of Culture and Communication.* www.culture.fr.

Freddy Silva, "Crop Circles: The Formative Years," *The Crop Circular.* www.lovely. clara.net.

———, "So It's All Done with Planks and Bits of String, Is It?" *The Crop Circular.* www.lovely.clara.net.

Stephen Wagner, "Crop Circles: Best Evidence," *About.* http://paranormal. about.com.

David Whitehouse, "Ice Age Star Map Discovered," *BBC News*, August 9, 2000. www.news.bbc.co.uk.

Wiltshire White Horses, "The Uffington White Horse." http://wiltshirewhite horses.org.uk.

Donna Yavelak, "Crop Circles: A Deeper Look," *Foundation for Paranormal Research.* www.paranormalresearchon line.com.

Helmut Zetti, "Tiahuanaco and the Deluge," *Catastrophism and Ancient History*, vol. VI, part 2, July 1984. www.thule.org.

Index

Picture Credits

About the Author

John F. Grabowski is a native of Brooklyn, New York. He holds a bachelor's degree in psychology from City College of New York and a master's degree in educational psychology from Teacher's College, Columbia University. He has been a teacher for thirty-three years, as well as a freelance writer, specializing in the fields of sports, education, and comedy. His body of published work includes forty-five books; a nationally syndicated sports column; consultation on several math textbooks; articles for newspapers, magazines, and the programs of professional sports teams; and comedy material sold to Jay Leno, Joan Rivers, Yakov Smirnoff, and numerous other comics. He and his wife Patricia live in Staten Island with their daughter Elizabeth.